OFF-ROADING

OFF-ROADING
RACING AND RIDING

IRWIN STAMBLER

G. P. PUTNAM'S SONS
NEW YORK

Acknowledgments

I am indebted to a number of people and organizations for assistance in the preparation of this book. In particular, I would like to thank: Deke Houlgate and John Houlgate, Deke Houlgate Enterprises; Mickey Thompson and Mickey Thompson Entertainment Group; Don Flamm and Ford Motor Company; SCORE International; Mint Hotel, Las Vegas; Chuck Burlingame and Toyota Motor Sales U.S.A.; United Four-Wheel Drive Associations; American Motorcyclist Association; Chrysler Corporation; General Motors Corporation; Nissan Motor Corporation U.S.A. (Datsun); Subaru of America, Inc.; American Motors Corporation; Yamaha Motor Corporation U.S.A.; FWD Corporation; American Honda Motor Company; Bilstein Corporation of America; Harley Davidson Division of AMF Corporation; Suzuki Motors; Kawasaki Company; Maico Motorcycles; and Goodyear Tire and Rubber Company.

Copyright © 1984 by Irwin Stambler
All rights reserved. Published simultaneously in
Canada by General Publishing Co. Limited, Toronto.
Printed in the United States of America
First Impression
Book design by Mike Suh

Library of Congress Cataloging in Publication Data

Stambler, Irwin, date.
Off-roading.
Includes index.
Summary: An introduction to the racing of jeeps, vans, pickup trucks, dune buggies, and other four-wheel-drive and specialized vehicles on beaches, deserts, natural routes, and specially constructed dirt tracks.
1. All terrain vehicle racing—Juvenile literature. 2. All terrain vehicles—Juvenile literature. [1. All terrain vehicle racing. 2. All terrain vehicles]
I. Title.
GV1037.S73   1984   796.7   84-8346
ISBN 0-399-21144-6

CONTENTS

1	OFF-ROAD COMES OF AGE	7
2	FOCUS ON FOUR-BY-FOURS	24
3	PICKING AN OFF-ROAD CYCLE	42
4	DO'S AND DON'TS OF OFF-ROADING	56
5	OFF-ROAD RACING THRILLS	73
6	GRASS-ROOTS OFF-ROADING	91
	PHOTOGRAPHS	105
	OFF-ROAD CLUBS AND ASSOCIATIONS	120
	INDEX	125

1
OFF-ROAD COMES OF AGE

In a remote, sparsely populated area of the United States, a long line of jeeps, vans, pickup trucks and dune buggies moves into place for a weekend of camping and hill-climb competition.

On sandy beaches and barren desert areas, riders on odd-looking balloon-tired three- or four-wheeled motorcycles roar over flat patches of sand or bounce over sand dunes with the greatest of ease.

On specially constructed dirt tracks in large stadiums and on treacherous, winding, long-distance natural routes, heavy-duty motorcycles and specially prepared cars and trucks fight for momentary glory and, in many cases, increasingly attractive purses in amateur and professional races.

It's all part of off-roading, an activity that, in terms of dollars spent and people involved, has rivaled rock concerts and video games in popularity since the 1970s. In fact, at the end of the 1970s and in the early 1980s, this sport brought growing sales of dirt bikes and four-wheel-drive automotive vehicles, providing at least one bright spot in the near-depression that had hit the private transportation field. As off-road entrepreneur and champion driver Mickey Thompson noted, "The fact that manufacturers, distributors and dealers selling products for pickups, four-wheel drives and dune buggies find themselves involved in the fastest growing segment of the automotive parts and accessories aftermarket [that is, parts and systems car owners buy to "jazz up" or improve their vehicles after they've left the dealer's lot] is really exciting."

The fact that off-roading really came into its own as a recreation and sport in the 1970s didn't mean it was a new pursuit. When you consider that the term "off-roading" simply means operating on unprepared roadways or trackless areas, you realize that this is the way things were before motorcycles and cars were invented. Back when mules, horses and animal-drawn vehicles were the main means of transportation, almost all pathways beyond major towns and cities were dirt. This held true even in the early days of the motor car. Asphalt and concrete roadways came along in the twentieth century to meet the needs and speed potential of high-performance passenger cars and trucks.

In a way, the mushrooming network of paved roads and impersonal superhighways helped bring about the renewed interest in off-road operations. In the years after World War II, sprawling cities beset by heavy traffic and lung-choking smog made many people subconsciously long for ways of escaping, for finding new personal freedom at least for a while. Motorcycles able to withstand the jolts and difficulties of back-country areas offered one way of doing this, although the number of people who could take part in dirt-bike trips was necessarily limited by the rigors of the travel involved.

Gradually, alternatives came along in the automotive category based on the use of four-wheel drive and the design of rugged vehicles that could take the pounding of off-road driving without breaking down or getting stuck. Starting in 1960, with the introduction of International Harvester Company's Scout, United States and foreign car builders began to provide off-road cars having both off-road reliability and passenger comfort. Previous to that, off-road vehicles like the redoubtable Willys Jeep gave dependable back-country performance, but the rider often was bounced about with bone-jarring intensity. It didn't bother dyed-in-the-wool off-road pioneers, who often used the four-wheel-drive system more for job-related activities like cattle roundups or oil exploration, but it was a bit much for people out for recreation.

During the 1970s and '80s, however, major car and truck manufacturers came up with a series of improved designs that resulted in vehicles able to traverse rugged terrain while still giving a smooth ride and, by the early 1980s, not only were vans and pickup trucks available with smoothly operating four-wheel drive, but regular passenger cars and station wagons also were offered. These provided a combination of four-wheel drive for off-road and what amounts to a two-wheel-drive adaptation for on-road driving.

In case you're wondering what we mean by four-wheel drive (or, as car makers and users often describe it, 4×4), it simply means that power from the engine is transmitted to all four wheels of the vehicle. In cars designed only for roads, engine power is sent to only two of the four wheels, either the rear pair or the front pair, with the other two, in effect, turning freely. For a vehicle that is used only on paved roads, the two-wheel system is preferred. The reasons for this are that the drive system is simpler that way, and some of the technical difficulties that must be solved for a workable four-wheel-drive installation are avoided.

Also, the two-wheel design can run well using a less powerful engine than is needed for a good four-wheel-drive vehicle. For off-road, the extra traction provided by four-wheel drive is vital. By supplying power to both front and rear axles, the drive system makes it possible for the vehicle both to pull on the front two wheels and push on the rear two, which is the key to bouncing over rocks or bumps in the road without losing control, or successfully navigating through sand, mud, snow and water hazards.

While four-wheel drive is the key to practical off-road cars and trucks, such a system obviously isn't needed for two- and three-wheel motorcycles. By their nature, motorcycles are lightweight, typically carrying only one person and using small but highly efficient engines. The power-to-gross-weight ratio is much higher than for large automotive systems and, being smaller, motorcycles are more maneuverable. From the time motorcycles came into existence in the 1800s up to the present, they always have had inherently good off-road performance, though there are still significant differences between dirt bikes and pavement cycles.

As far as four-wheel drive is concerned, it isn't really new either. In truth, it is almost as old as the horseless carriage.

Although the first truly practical design was initiated by Four Wheel Drive Auto Company in Clintonville, Wisconsin, in 1908 (at least available records indicate that was the first practical system), several other four-wheel-drive vehicles were built years before that.

Records indicate three early automobile companies worked on such designs just after the turn of the century: the Columbia Automobile Company of Hartford, Connecticut (founded in 1897 with its name changed first to Columbia Auto & Electrical Vehicle Company in 1900, then to Electric Vehicle Company in 1901), the Aultman Motor Car Company of Canton, Ohio, and Cotta Motor Car Company of Rockford, Illinois. Which company actually demonstrated a four-wheel-drive vehicle first seems lost in the mists of time.

The Electric Vehicle design employed four-wheel drive to power a large five-ton truck. It used electric propulsion with four electric motors, one behind each wheel. The drive shaft of each motor turned metal chains which, in turn, rotated the wheels. The two front motors also provided some power through gears to a fifth wheel located under the driver's compartment. It was movement of that wheel that provided steering capability.

The Aultman design was also a truck. Indicating the many approaches for generating energy studied in the automobile's infancy, this system was based on a steam-driven engine. Since all the power in this case was from a single engine source rather than four different power plants as in the Electric Vehicle model, some way was needed to transmit the rotational movement from engine shaft to the wheels. When the Aultman people began to examine the situation, they realized there were problems if they tried to use a single shaft transmitting power to a single axle in the rear and a single one in the front on a four-wheel-drive system. The difficulty is due to the difference in velocity experienced by different wheels when the steering system is used for turning.

The approach taken by Aultman was to use a conventional rear axle, but have two axles on the front. One of those two front axles was used for steering and the other for driving the front wheels. Power from the steam engine was transmitted to the rear axle through a double chain system and through double-faced bevel gears that meshed with vertical gears at each end of the drive axle.

The Aultman, like the Electric Vehicle four-wheel-drive vehicle, was a five-ton truck, a portent of the immediate future for four-wheel drive which for much of its history was used essentially for truck propulsion, particularly for military trucks.

The Cotta design ranks as the ancestor of passenger type off-roaders, though its designers didn't have all-terrain use in mind; they were just experimenting with a possibly unique passenger model for those times. The car was the only one of the three intended to use a gasoline engine. Power from the engine was delivered to a specially devised central universal joint which, in turn, rotated the four wheels by means of separate drive chains. As far as we can tell, only one Cotta FWD car was built and the idea of four-wheel-drive passenger-car systems then lay dormant for decades.

None of the above three vehicles ever made it into production. Electric Vehicle Company did become one of the largest truck manufacturers of the early 1900s, but almost all of its vehicles had standard two-wheel drive.

It remained for a series of unplanned events in a small Wisconsin town to give rise to the forerunner of today's 4 × 4 boom. The first link in the chain came in the winter of 1905-06 when Clintonville blacksmiths Otto Zachow and William Besserdich, sensing the demise of much of their horseshoeing-based business, agreed to be the local agents for one of the major names in early automobile history, the Reo. Their first customer was Clintonville physician Dr. W. H. Finney.

One day, at a time when the dirt roads, though waterlogged from winter storms, were ice-firm under freezing winter temperatures, Zachow accompanied Finney on a drive to a nearby village. On the way back, the weather changed. Warm winds caused the ice and snow to begin to melt, turning stretches of the horse-and-buggy road into quagmires. The car got stuck in one boghole and no matter what the two men did, they couldn't budge it. They finally walked back to Clintonville and Finney had to wait until the dirt road dried out before he could reclaim his car.

The incident, the story goes, immediately made Zachow

start to consider if ways might be found to improve the Reo's foul-weather performance. However, for a long time nothing practical came to mind. He thought up a number of schemes, but discarded each one as being either unworkable or too expensive.

It wasn't until a year later that a way of doing it finally occurred to him. It was after he swerved off the road into a ravine during a trip to Appleton, Wisconsin. Fortunately, neither he nor his car was hurt. But when he faced the car into the slope that led back to the road and tried to move up, the unpowered front wheels just dug into the hillside. He gave that method up and pondered the matter. Suddenly he thought about trying to back up the slope. Since the rear wheels were the driving wheels, he reasoned, they would get their traction on the hillside and pull the rest of the car up. He turned the car around, put the transmission into reverse gear and pushed his foot down on the accelerator. The rear wheels took hold and the car moved up, up and finally back onto the road.

Zachow had rediscovered the principle of four-wheel drive, since in those days of relatively limited communications he hadn't ever heard of the prototypes made by companies like Electric Vehicle and Aultman. But he took things a step further by inventing a feasible way of dividing power from the single engine to the four wheels. He solved the problem by inventing a new kind of double-Y universal joint. The concept was suggested to him from observing the working principles of some of the mechanical threshers used by local farmers. In his blacksmith shop he fashioned the parts for the device, one in which the joint, located in the front of the vehicle, was installed in a ball and socket arrangement such that the wheels could rotate without interfering with the operation of the power-drive system.

Once he was sure his invention would work, Zachow asked local lawyer Walter Olen to file the appropriate patent application. This took a year to complete, so it wasn't until 1908 that Zachow felt ready to build his first four-wheel-drive prototype.

The model he selected was a Stanley Steamer, recently purchased by his old customer Dr. Finney. By the summer of

1908, Zachow and Besserdich had outfitted the large eight-passenger vehicle with Zachow's system and demonstrated that it would work to their own and Finney's satisfaction. Soon after, the three men put up the initial capital for the Badger Four Wheel Drive Auto Company. The name eventually was shortened to the Four Wheel Drive Auto Company.

It took almost six years of persistence and several reorganizations before the company met with success. By then the original partners had sold their interests and the company was headed by Walter Olen, the Clintonville lawyer who had filed the FWD patents for Zachow. In effect, though, it took a war for four-wheel drive to get started. The onset of World War I fueled interest among military leaders at home and abroad in truck designs that could operate reliably under battlefield conditions. First the British and then the United States armies ordered production quantities of Four Wheel Drive Auto Company three- and five-ton trucks. During World War I, the firm turned out thousands of those trucks, which became vital elements in Allied transportation networks.

In the years following the war military orders dropped off, but by then the Clintonville four-wheel-drive system was accepted as a conventional option for vehicles employed in rugged service. The company turned to production of specialized models, such as snow plows and fire engines, and is still active in these areas today.

The military again became a factor in four-wheel-drive progress during World War II, this time in small-sized vehicles. The Light Command and Reconnaissance Car, better known as the "Jeep," became a familiar sight in U.S. Army operations all over the world. There are various stories about where the name came from, but most likely it derives from the army classification of this type of vehicle as general purpose, sometimes shortened to the acronym GP. It didn't take long for soldiers to turn the "GP" into the sound-alike "jeep."

The firm that almost always comes to mind among four-wheel-drive fans when the Jeep is mentioned is Willys Overland Company. Actually, the first working vehicle to meet the army's general specification for a small four-wheel-drive vehicle wasn't made by Willys, but by the American Bantam Company of Butler, Pennsylvania. The first Bantam car, weighing over 1,800 pounds with a wheelbase of about 80 inches and an engine turning out more than 85 foot-pounds of torque (the force or combination of forces producing a twisting or rotating motion), was completed and demonstrated in the fall of 1940. The initial production order was placed with that company.

However, also in the competition was Willys Overland and Ford Motor Company. Because these were larger companies with greater resources in money and production facilities, they soon received the really large orders that flowed from the U.S. military as the country became involved in World War II on all fronts. During the first half of the 1940s, a stream of Jeeps came off the Willys line in Toledo, Ohio, and from Ford plants in Michigan.

The first Willys Jeep, designated the model MA, had a four-cylinder gasoline engine capable of turning out up to 61 horsepower. That engine, which could provide 103 foot-pounds of torque at 2,000 revolutions per minute, had an extra power margin that gave it an advantage over the other Jeep designs for operation under severe conditions. (By comparison, the first Ford model, designated the GP, had a maximum rating for its engine of 40 horsepower, while the Bantam's maximum power was 46 horsepower.) For this reason, by war's end, the Willys product had overshadowed its competitors to the point that today many people forget any models other than the Willys MA and slightly improved Willys MB were used in U.S. World War II operations. Actually, both Ford and Willys built hundreds of thousands of service Jeeps in the 1940s. Most of Ford's production was an upgraded version designated the GPW. The latter matched the Willys performance by replacing the original Ford engine with the higher horsepower power plant devised for the first MAs. Hence the "W" in GPW stands for "Willys."

Military orders during World War II, of course, didn't just go for reconnaissance car FWDs. There were plenty of requirements for trucks, ambulances and other large vehicles that profited from four-wheel-drive off-road capability. Every major automobile manufacturer turned out some of those. For post-war civilian use, where there increasingly were excellent all-weather roads in all parts of the United States and Canada, there wasn't much call for four-wheel-drive trucks. On the other hand, many war veterans, who had been entranced by the back-road potential of Jeeps, were eager to buy used or new models for recreation or job use. Many commercial operations wanted them too; Jeeps were naturals for things like monitoring remote utility lines, searching for oil and gas deposits and small-scale hauling of cargo. It wasn't a mass market at the time, but it was good enough to provide good civilian business for Willys when the war was over. Other companies, like Ford and Chrysler, offered pickup trucks and vans equipped with four-wheel drive based on technology developed during the war years.

So the military again had played a pivotal role in the progress of off-roading. It took some time before off-road systems evolved into the sophisticated variety of designs that account for today's booming four-wheel-drive market, but the wheels, so to speak, had been set in motion with the army Jeep.

In much the same way, military needs in the United States and abroad played a role in the saga of the motorcycle. It wasn't too long after motorcycles were invented that they made their way into armies around the world. Long before the first four-wheel-drive vehicles came off truck production lines, most armies had couriers who made their way over back roads and through trackless terrain on heavy-duty cycles. During World War I, big-gun mechanics in the U.S. Army used off-road type motorcycles to get to gun emplacements that needed repair or maintenance.

In somewhat of a reverse way, innovations resulting from military defeat contributed to the rise of the Japanese motorcycle industry that today is the dominant force in both on- and off-road two- and three-wheelers. Devastated both economically and physically by its World War II setbacks, the Japanese population was in desperate need of efficient, low-cost personal transportation. A Japanese engineer named Soichiro Honda reasoned that a motorized bicycle might find a ready market for this need.

Honda bought a batch of small two-cycle engines that the

Japanese Imperial Army had used to power communications equipment and adapted them to bicycles. The motorized bikes literally sold like hot cakes in the vehicle-less period after Japan surrendered. When surplus two-cycle engines ran out, the company built its own 50 cubic centimeter (cc) engine (the figure refers to the engine displacement, the volume in the cylinders available for compression and explosion of the fuel-air mixture) and, a little while later, a 100 cc engine that was used in Honda's first true motorcycles. Other cycle makers in Japan also began to take advantage of the seemingly insatiable appetite of their countrymen for motorcycles. A little more than a decade after the end of World War II, the Japanese firms realized a similar market awaited them overseas.

Though American and European motorcycle manufacturers had a lead in bikes suitable for off-road racing and riding, it didn't take Japanese firms long to catch up. By the early 1960s, typical Honda, Yamaha, Suzuki, et al., lines included dirt bikes, and riders using some of those models were doing quite well in events ranging from punishing off-road long-distance competitions to international motocross races. In the late 1970s, it was the Japanese motorcycle industry that opened up some new horizons for off-road enthusiasts with widespread introduction of new series of balloon-tired three- and four-wheel cycles (also referred to as ATVs, or All Terrain Vehicles).

In both four-wheel-drive vehicles and motorcycles, off-road racing contributed to the evolution of equipment that helped make today's boom possible. Almost as soon as the first automobiles were invented, owners and/or drivers were challenging each other to races or time trials. The same held true earlier when bicycles first appeared and, a while later, when the motorcycles that evolved from the bicycles came along. In all cases, competition inspired tinkering with components or making aerodynamic changes to gain an edge for one party over the others.

While off-road motorcycles were involved in many racing events from before the beginning of the century, the technical complexities of four-wheel drive hindered its immediate use in race vehicles. That doesn't mean there were no off-road races for four-wheel-drive vehicles. The automobile hardly had been invented before drivers of "hot" cars were challenging each other. By necessity, the early races were run mainly on dirt because that was about the only kind of road available. Over the years from the turn of the century to the early 1930s, plenty of informal off-road racing took place in rural areas. In the 1930s, off-road pickup truck races were common in the West and Southwest. However, these were two-wheel drive vehicles and the drivers tried to race on stretches of flat dirt where problems of mud and sand were avoided as much as possible.

But the steps that would lead to the more wide-open off-road races of post–World War II decades were beginning to be taken by the end of the 1920s. By the start of the 1930s, Four Wheel Drive Auto Company was working on Indianapolis-type 4×4 designs, and cars using this approach competed in a number of Indy 500 races. In 1936, with the famed Maury Rose at the wheel, one of those racers finished fourth at Indy and might have won if not for a last-minute pit stop for fuel.

In the years just after World War II, off-road racing vehicles derived from some of those Four Wheel Drive Auto Company models held their own in several hill-climb type events. But by then all kinds of 4×4 models were in production for civilian use, the Willys Jeep in particular enjoying wide popularity for off-road competition. By the late 1940s, other manufacturers were producing a range of 4×4s from Jeep-size models to full-size pickups that also were soon adapted for all kinds of racing challenges. Besides that, off-road enthusiasts started making new kinds of off-road vehicles from models originally made for two-wheel-drive use. In time, races like the Mint 400 and Baja 1000 amounted to a series of simultaneous races embracing many different categories from motorcycles to trucks rather than single competitions.

One of the most popular off-road racing families evolved from the German-built Volkswagen, a car originally designed for use on conventional roads. In time, off-road buffs realized that the VW design lent itself to modification that resulted in an excellent off-road vehicle. Some of those conversions, which eventually became available in various kit forms, were used for recreational purposes. But others were designed specifically for racing. Known as "dune buggies," these provided many exciting moments in off-road competition from the start of the 1960s right up to the current decade.

It's generally agreed among dune-buggy historians that the first such conversions were made around 1960. According to *Four Wheeler* magazine, Scott McKenzie of San Fernando, California, was one of the pioneers, perhaps "the" pioneer, in the birth of the dune-buggy concept. After observing that the normal VW production car had a very rugged suspension, well suited to withstand the sudden shocks and high vibration levels of unprepared driving surfaces, he figured that it might be modified for that kind of use. He also decided that, by removing the heavy metal body, he could get a vehicle capable of getting 40 miles per gallon of gas rather than the 25-30 mpg of the regular VW.

In addition, the VW gear is well adapted to the rapid shifting needed to operate a car over quickly changing land contours. The combination of transmission design plus the VW's independent suspension provided both high maneuverability and relatively high speeds under back-country conditions.

McKenzie and other early VW buggy fans kept costs down by getting the parts they needed from junkyards. After removing the passenger shell from the old car, they cut the frame and shortened it 11 to 12 inches to reach a wheelbase of around 84 inches, only a little longer than the original jeep. The reason for reducing the wheelbase is that it provides much better handling conditions for off-road running, whether on loose dirt or sand. Front wheels usually weren't altered, but in the back, rims for larger tires were welded onto the axle system and special low-pressure "floppy" tires mounted on the rims. Then the structure needed for other vehicle requirements, such as seat supports and steering, was rebuilt using aluminum tubing for minimum weight. And, of course, four-wheel drive typically was incorporated into the system.

Such stripped-down vehicles were excellent for those who liked to rough it in remote areas or for the growing number of buggy race fans. As years passed, many versions were developed using plastic bodies and tops for drivers who just liked the sporty look of dune buggies and weren't interested in racing. This was an example of how off-road racing provided concepts that found favor for off-road pleasure-type applications. Among better known models available in kit form or fully assembled in the mid 1980s were various designs of the Magnum family produced by Chenowth Racing Products, El Cajon, California, the Funco Hustler developed by Funco Race Cars, Ontario, California, and the Chaparral made by Palmer Speed Equipment, Phoenix, Arizona.

Meanwhile, improvements in off-road racing dune buggies continued at a steady pace. For instance, designers and race drivers realized that using carefully streamlined plastic body sections could more than make up in reduced aerodynamic drag for any slight increase in gross weight if those were used in preference to a stripped down version. Also helping to improve performance was the availability of more powerful engines than the original passenger car power plant. Using the improved VW engines of the 1970s, for instance, such as the 65 horsepower 1600S unit with twin carburetors, permitted reaching speeds of over 100 miles per hour in well-designed buggies. Of course, such speeds are good for dirt-track racing, but don't mean much in true back-country competition, other than that, all other things being equal, a more powerful engine should give one vehicle an edge over another.

The same sort of improvising and updating that vastly improved dune-buggy performance over the years occurred in other categories as well. The results achieved by top racers in all classes of racing in the 1980s almost made the vehicles of only a decade or so before look like they operated in slow motion.

Providing inducements for those trends were the developments in organized off-road racing. In the years right after World War II, particularly in the West and Southwest, increasing numbers of off-road 4 × 4s and motorcycles raced each other informally or vied in setting new time marks for long-distance off-road journeys. A major early attraction was the mostly uninhabited wild expanse of the finger of Mexican territory stretching south from the California border known as Baja California. Initially there weren't organized events; if someone wanted to try to set a record, he just went off and did it. If individuals wanted to race each other on the Baja, they figured out a course and away they went. But as word of some of those feats reached more and more off-road fans, eventually it set the stage for larger, better-planned competitions.

One of the first widely publicized achievements came in 1962 when cyclists Dave Ekins and Bill Robertson, Jr., rode a pair of Honda 250-cc bikes the 900 miles from Tijuana to La Paz in 19 hours, 34 minutes. As the 1960s went by, drivers of various off-road four-wheel-drive vehicles also took up the challenge. In April 1967, Bruce Meyers and Ted Mangels set a mark of 34 hours, 45 minutes from La Paz to Tijuana in a Manx VW dune buggy, a mark cut to 31 hours three months later by drivers Spence Murray and Ralph Poole.

The racing instincts of many individuals aroused and inspired a man named Ed Pearlman to form the first formal off-road racing group, the National Off-Road Racing Association. That group sponsored the first Mexican 1000, later called the Baja 1000. The following year the Mint Hotel in Las Vegas started its own race, the Mint 400, still a premiere annual event.

Because of the many types of vehicles that could take part in off-road racing, the interest of vehicle builders, designers and racers was whetted. From the late 1960s on, many members of more traditional types of racing became aware of the fun and excitement promised by off-road competition. People like Indy champion Parnelli Jones and drag-race world-speed-record challenger Mickey Thompson were early converts.

Thompson in particular soon understood that off-road not only was a racer's delight, but could have a bright future as a spectator sport. In 1973 he helped form a new group called Short Course Off-Road Enterprises, or SCORE, which went about setting up rules for the sport and establishing racing categories. By the 1980s, the group's acronym became a better description of SCORE's activities than the full title, because the organization by then sponsored not only short course races, but long grueling contests. The latter category included the Baja 1000 and Baja International for which the Mexican government invited SCORE to begin handling organizational chores in the mid 1970s. Appropriately, Mickey Thompson won the Baja 1000 in 1982.

By the mid 1980s, SCORE was presiding over a regular series of major races that, taken together, provided room for several dozen different racing classes. These included divisions based on vehicle performance capabilities for dune buggies, motorcycles, three wheelers, full-size and mini-pickups, stock VW sedans, etc. (These are discussed in more detail in Chapter 5.) The different categories offered opportunities for all manner of off-road enthusiasts from the relative novice to the highly skilled professional driver. As the years went by, the professionals not only were attracted by the enjoyment of such races, but by steadily growing amounts of prize money.

Thus a typical event series might feature racing greats like Thompson, Indy star Gordon Johncock and NASCAR stock car ace Roger Mears as well as someone from the local garage. Major races drew international sponsors like the Pernod beverage firm from France and overseas drivers and celebrities. In the November 1982 Baja race the cast included 29-year-old Mark Thatcher, son of British prime minister Margaret Thatcher, who entered the race using a 4×4 pickup with co-driver being off-road veteran John Randall of Mesa, Arizona. Thatcher, who had gained national press coverage the previous January when his car broke down in the Sahara Desert during a 10,000-mile Paris-to-Dakar motor rally (because he wasn't heard from for some time there were fears he might have suffered harm), suggested the Baja might be a good windup to his racing efforts. "I've had it in the back of my mind for some time to race in the Baja. . . . I may decide to drive in some local races at home, but this is it for my career."

An example of the way off-road could serve as a proving ground for automotive designers was the association of driving ace Roger Mears with student engineers from California Polytechnic State University at San Luis Obispo. For a SCORE-sponsored event at Riverside Raceway, California, in the summer of 1981, Mears agreed to drive a mini-pickup truck modified by a student team as part of its mechanical engineering studies. The students, headed by Bryan Kudela, worked on a 1980 three-quarter-ton longbed pickup given the university by Toyota of America. The modified vehicle, entirely designed and constructed at the school, featured quadruple shock capacity for each wheel, a full floating rear end, four-wheel disc brakes and a roll cage made from urethane plastic. To improve performance of the five stock 2200- and 2400-cc engines readied for the race, the student team increased the compression ratio to 11:1, installed larger carburetors and high-performance cams and pistons, and balanced and blueprinted all parts.

Thus off-road events serve as a proving ground for new skills and new ideas. Besides amateur groups and local mechanics, major auto companies obviously learn a lot about new systems from shock absorbers to engines from the punishment of off-road races. Some of this finds its way into future recreational off-road vehicles as well as conventional two-wheel-drive designs.

In special events like the SCORE Off-Road Equipment Show the loop is closed between racing and recreational off-road activities. The tens of thousands of people who come to shows of this kind often find improvements for use on their own vehicles or get ideas from the exhibits for getting better off-road performance from their equipment. Some attendees, of course, simply want to see close up some of the impressive racing machines they cheered for at off-road contests, typically the short closed-course ones.

Mickey Thompson had expected that such sport fan interest would increase sharply from the short course races he sponsored starting in the mid 1970s. His idea was to adopt arenas like the 100,000-seat Los Angeles Coliseum and the course at the Los Angeles County Fairgrounds in Pomona for off-road competition. By carefully setting up dirt tracks that matched, in a compressed amount of space, the challenges of natural off-road courses, he gave onlookers the chance to see such races from start to finish, something not possible on the sprawling Baja 1000, Mint 400 or Parker 400 layouts. In 1982, as he watched 4 × 4s practice before one of the races held on the Los Angeles County Fairgrounds off-road course with upwards of 70,000 people in attendance, he told a reporter, "This has been my dream. This is a ten-year dream coming to life right here. We're putting off-road racing, the most fun, the most exciting racing there is, on a great, permanent track and where you can be comfortable in the best facility for racing in the United States."

It echoed what he had said about the SCORE equipment show. "It's fun to be part of something relatively new. When my partner Alex Xydias and I formed [their off-road enterprise company], we did it with a great deal of enthusiasm. We were both fortunate many years ago to be among the pioneers of the performance industry, and I can truthfully say it's meant a great deal to us. We made many lasting friendships in the early days and it's still fun to 'bench race' about it today. We saw that same opportunity in the off-road field. We saw many similarities in the current development of off-roading to our experience in hot rodding years ago and felt sure we could put that experience to good use in helping the off-road industry continue its growth and success. As for the future . . . the size of the SCORE show itself is one indication of what's happening. In all honesty, the show is larger than we anticipated and more than twice the size that many industry observers expected it to be. It proves off-road is here to stay as a major sport and recreation and it's going to give a lot of pleasure to a large part of the public in years to come."

2
FOCUS ON FOUR-BY-FOURS

While there has been steadily growing interest over the years in two- and three-wheel systems, there's no doubt that the "boom" area in recent times has been in 4 × 4 automotive vehicles. In the late 1970s the demand for light trucks became so great that all truck builders in the United States and abroad were hard pressed to keep up with it. In 1978 and 1979, roughly 30 percent of all industry sales were for new pickup truck models, a category that accounted for only a fraction of the total output in the 1960s.

In the 1980s, popularity of light trucks remained high and this mainly four-wheel-drive group was augmented by an attraction among buyers of vans and passenger cars to vehicles equipped with "part-time" four-wheel drive. This development, made possible by great strides in technology that got underway in the 1960s, offered the user the flexibility of being able to have two- or four-wheel drive "on demand" without losing any of the comforts or capabilities expected in a regular two-wheel-drive model. Equally important, the dual-drive capability was made available with very little effect on the overall price. Some car buyers liked the idea of being able to take the family car into off-road recreation sites; others who lived in places where winter conditions were severe liked the four-wheel-drive system's powerful performance in ice and snow.

For the best four-wheel-drive operation, well designed subsystems—good shock absorbers, correct tire selection, efficient engines—are important. But the most important factor in the evolution of 4 × 4s is finding good ways to transmit power to all four wheels. So before considering some of the vehicles that now use four-wheel drive, let's concentrate on getting a good understanding of the principles and problems involved.

For most of automotive history, the majority of vehicles have used two-wheel drive where the engine's power is transmitted to only one pair of wheels, usually the rear wheels, although in recent years the trend has been to the front wheels. As we pointed out in the first chapter, two-wheel drive works well for paved highway conditions and generally requires a less complicated mechanism than for four-wheel drive.

The main consideration in developing workable four-wheel drives—and to a lesser extent two-wheel drives—is coping with the different speed requirements of the wheels when turning or when moving over uneven ground. If you draw a diagram of a car going around a curve, plotting the arcs covered by each of the four wheels as they go from the start of the curve to the head of a straight portion of roadway, you'll quickly see that each wheel goes through a different distance. This means that each wheel must rotate at a different speed to negotiate the turn successfully. If this doesn't happen, say if two wheels were solidly attached to the same axle, one wheel would, in effect, be dragged part of the way causing extra wear on the tires and placing increased strain on the axle. In time, under those conditions, tires would wear out rapidly or stresses would build up in the transmission-axle system that could cause failures in some of the parts.

In two-wheel drive systems the situation is avoided in two ways. For the driven wheels, the transmission employs a series of gears in what is known as a differential. That is, the gears operate in such a way that during turns or other modes involving uneven wheel speeds the engine power is divided up so that more is sent to the wheel that must move faster than to the other one. An axle system where this kind of power division occurs is called a live axle. In effect, there is a double axle with one part attached to one wheel and the second part to the other. The second way in which problems are avoided is the use of a "dead axle" system for the pair of wheels that doesn't receive engine power. In this case, the wheels are not rigidly attached to the axle, but are allowed to rotate freely on the ends of the axle. Under those circumstances, each wheel can rotate at the appropriate speed during a turn.

For four-wheel drive, both front and rear axles must be "driven." Obviously, for starters, this calls for having two transmission/differential systems, one to send part of the power to the rear pair and a second to provide some of the power to the front pair. Actually, the second differential not only may have to divide power properly between two wheels, it also may have to reverse the direction of the original engine output. This is true for the conventional front-to-back engine arrangement where the crankshaft rotation transmits power in one direction only. A number of recent vehicle designs, though, use a trans-axle engine arrangement—that is, the engine's main axis runs from side to side of the vehicle rather than front to back. In this case, the crankshaft is at right angles to driveshaft directions and reversal isn't needed.

Before discussing four-wheel-drive design in more detail, we might digress for a moment to point out that the way power is transmitted and divided in all these systems mainly depends on various arrangements of gears. Gears are mechanical devices in which the number, size and spacing of projections called teeth determine the ratios of power output. Meshing gears with different properties can allow for division of output referred to as "step-up" and "step-down" ratios. For a step-down ratio of 5-2, for example, it means that if the input speed is 50 revolutions per minute (rpm), the output speed from the gear assembly would be 20 rpm. For step-up, the situation would be reversed.

While having two transmissions provides a way to run a vehicle with two live axles, it causes problems in steering. On a two-wheel-drive design, the steering wheel works typically by moving the dead axle. When that axle becomes live, some way to steer is still needed. This has been accomplished by using a special joint arrangement, usually a U-joint system, so that the power and turning operations of the axle are isolated from each other.

As far back as the Four Wheel Drive Auto Company's infancy, the two-transmission, special steering-axle joint installation had been demonstrated. Still, this did not avoid some serious drawbacks that for a long time limited wider use of four-wheel drive. One of the two main difficulties is what is known as "breakaway."

Breakaway refers to a condition where a driving wheel loses traction. This can happen, for instance, when one wheel hits a patch of ice, an oil slick, etc., while the other one has solid footing. As the one wheel starts spinning, the other wheel stops moving forward. This can take place with a four-wheel as well as a two-wheel-drive system, although the four-wheel-drive can in many such cases perform much better than a two-wheel drive. That is, with four-wheel drive, often when one wheel spins, the other three have enough traction to move the vehicle out of the problem area. But situations can arise in a four-wheel-drive system where both wheels on one side hit a slick or other obstacle that immobilizes both pairs of wheels.

The driver's "knee jerk" reaction is to push down on the accelerator to try to get the vehicle moving by brute force. This often results in the wheel or wheels on one side taking far more load than it or they are designed for, which can have devastating effects, resulting in broken gears or failed bearings. If this situation is bad for a two-wheel drive system, it can be twice as serious for a 4×4, which has many more parts and connections.

Eventually, designers came up with a way of avoiding the problem by incorporating a special gear arrangement. This involves adding types of gears known as worm and crown gears whose teeth slant along the gear surface rather than being straight up and down. By arranging them in the proper relationship to each other it is possible to have a system where the worm gear will drive the crown gear under normal conditions to provide differential power to the wheels. However, if one wheel loses traction, the worm gear no longer can drive the crown gear but the latter can drive the worm gear. In effect, this "locks" the system to give what amounts to a solid axle. When this happens, the spinning of the wheel on the slick surface forces the other wheel to turn as well, giving traction to make the vehicle move past the obstacle.

The second major problem that had to be solved for practical four-wheel drive is called "driveline windup." This is a front-to-back problem caused by the fact that, unlike a two-wheel-drive vehicle, all the wheels on a 4×4 are connected through the driveshaft to the differential. During turns or other maneuvers, since all four wheels want to turn at different speeds, they introduce forces into the drivetrain that need to be relieved in some way to avoid damage. You might compare what happens to the way a spring works in a wind-up clock or toy. As you turn the key, more and more "potential" energy is stored in the spring material. It's this energy whose release makes the toy move or the clock hands rotate. If this spring is overwound it reaches the point where it can't hold any more energy and it will break down in some way.

For a vehicle, in off-road operation there's no problem because as its tires hit depressions or bumps one or more wheels come free of the ground and the system "unwinds" to get rid of the extra load. On conventional paved roads this usually doesn't happen and the driveline can become more and more stressed until some kind of sudden failure takes place.

One answer to this came early in the truck field. Designers at Walker Truck Company got the idea of putting what amounts to a third differential (with still more gearing) inside the second power transfer case. This system uses worm gears to allow a locking differential action for cases of driveline windup as well as breakaway. It works quite well, but is expensive and thus didn't find favor for small trucks or passenger vehicles.

The initial answer of the engineering team at Willys Overland for Jeep models during World War II and for postwar civilian models was to use a "shift-out" mechanism. The driver was provided with a second lever in addition to the regular gearshift lever. Moved in one direction the lever moved a shift rod assembly that disengaged the front wheels; moved in the other direction it engaged them. When the front wheels were disengaged, the car effectively became a two-wheel-drive system. The problem was that the driver sometimes forgot to do that, opening the door to the excessive forces already mentioned.

As use of off-road vehicles for extended highway use became popular, Jeep engineers and other vehicle builders developed alternatives to the shift-out approach. This took the form of installing an additional transmission, but one simpler and less foolproof than the one used in the Walker Truck. The tradeoff meant the system wasn't quite as reliable as the truck system, but it was much less expensive. Called a "drop box" or "power divider," this system used a series of gears to "drop" the power from the initial input to the transmission to the levels needed by each wheel for a turn or other directional change. As the 1960s and 1970s went by, designers continually worked on improvements and variations of this "third transmission" approach until systems evolved that were not only relatively inexpensive, but also highly reliable. These are widely used in trucks and cars with 4 × 4 capabilities in the 1980s.

In the late 1970s and early 1980s, a wide range of models that offered either full-time or part-time four-wheel drive were produced. For typical full-time four-wheel drive, an operator had the option of having the front and rear axles running essentially independently of each other or coordinating their movements for more demanding off-road situations.

Ford Motor Company in its *Light Truck Buying Guide* described its 4 × 4 systems: "Full-time four-wheel drive has a transfer case with an inter-axle differential which delivers power to both axles while compensating for differences between front and rear axle speeds. The driver can lock the axles together by moving the transfer case shift lever located inside the vehicle. Full-time four-wheel drive vehicles allow a low lock and high lock position. Low lock is used for extra traction and power, high lock for extra traction only.

"In part-time four-wheel drive, the transfer case does not adjust power between the front and rear axles, but provides constant and equal power to both axles. The axles turn at the same speed regardless of the terrain, therefore providing maximum pulling and pushing power. The vehicle can be operated with power to one axle only, providing two-wheel drive, or to both front and rear axles when four-wheel drive is needed. A feature called free-wheeling front hubs disconnects the front wheels from the axle. These hand-operated clutches, one on each front wheel, are designed to engage or disengage the front wheels from the axle.

"The part-time four-wheel-drive system requires the driver to get out of the vehicle and to manually engage or disengage both of the front hubs, depending on the mode of driving desired. However, the system has the ability to use conventional two-wheel drive for normal driving conditions. And this helps eliminate wear on the front axle and save on fuel consumption."

The typical dual-mode car or truck of the 1960s and 1970s required the manual engagement/disengagement of the front wheel hubs described above. But the obvious appeal of change mechanisms that could be operated from inside the vehicle led to intensive research and development studies among auto manufacturers for systems that could offer that provision. The availability of better materials, improved gear systems and solid state electronics for vastly improved control of vehicle devices helped bring about a steady trend to such easier-to-run installations in the late 1970s and early 1980s. Among the pioneers in that field were American Motors and Subaru, both of whom introduced passenger cars where the change from two-wheel to four-wheel drive and vice versa could be done just by flipping a switch on the dashboard.

American Motors first offered that method, called the Select-Drive System, on its Eagle series beginning in 1980. As of the mid-1980s, the Eagle was produced in three separate body styles: a four-door sedan, four-door wagon and SX-4 liftback. The engine for all of these is a 2.5 liter, 151 cubic-inch-displacement (CID) four-cylinder power plant with a 4.2 liter, 258 CID six-cylinder engine offered as an option. The SX-4 could be obtained with an automatic transmission with either size engine, while the other two models were available as automatics only with the six-cylinder power plant. An indication that Eagle models were far different in style from the rough and rugged cars of four-wheel drive's early days is this list of some of the other features or options offered: power steering, power brakes, glass-belted radial tires, vinyl reclining regular or bucket seats, full woodgrain instrument panel overlay, styled wheel covers, bumper guards, extra-quiet insulation, dual horns, air conditioning, tinted glass, rear-window defogger, power windows, tilt steering wheel, remote-control outside mirrors and electronically tuned AM-FM cassette stereo radio.

Beginning in 1983, American Motors introduced a "full-time 4WD/2WD" system similar to the Eagle's called Selec-Trac as a standard item on the Jeep Wagoneer and as an option for the Cherokee and J-10 pickup truck models. The new system was offered only with an automatic transmission. Discussing the new system, an American Motors official said, "This succeeds Jeep Quadra-Trac, a full-time 4WD system, which was itself revolutionary when it was introduced by Jeep Corporation in 1973. With the introduction of Selec-Trac, Jeep Wagoneer, Cherokee and Jeep J-10 will be the only sports utility vehicles in the industry—domestic or import—to offer a system capable of full-time 4WD operation. Additionally, Jeep continues to offer part-time 4WD and thus remains the only manufacturer offering two separate transfer case systems, both capable of 4WD and 2WD operation."

The main difference between Selec-Trac and the Eagle's Select-Drive, company engineers pointed out, was Selec-Trac's addition of "a low range, or two-speed capability in the transfer case for added torque when required. This low-range mode can be activated only when the Jeep vehicle is in 4WD. A sequential lockout system within the transfer case prevents activation of low range when the vehicle is in 2WD. Low range can be activated by a floor-mounted lever next to the driver."

To change from two-wheel drive to four-wheel drive or back in these vehicles requires the driver to stop and activate the switch mounted on the instrument panel. The rest happens automatically. If you had one of these vehicles, you wouldn't have to get out and adjust the wheel hubs. The instrument design includes a safety catch to avoid accidental movement of the Selec-Trac switch.

Naturally, while the operator only has to flick the dashboard switch with a finger to change driving modes, a lot takes place elsewhere in the vehicle. For instance, if you chose the 2WD mode, engineers note, the first thing to happen would be for the transfer case to shift into two-wheel drive. "Then the front drivetrain is released from the freely turning front wheels by a vacuum-actuated disconnect device built into the front axle assembly. This vacuum-actuated disconnect spline clutch, which is disengaged in the 4WD mode, releases torque to the left axle shaft in the 2WD mode.

"Because the axle differential always serves to equalize torque between the right and left axle shafts, the release of the left axle shaft torque, allowing it to turn freely, also relieves the right axle torque. The single spline clutch, therefore, relieves both left and right front axle torque from the hypoid gear set just as effectively as if both sides had been disconnected individually."

For the full-time four-wheel-drive mode, the above operation is reversed automatically so that all four wheels deliver engine power to the road.

American Motors engineers also noted that the Selec-Trac transfer case "includes a mechanical shifter that allows a spline clutch, located on the transfer case main shaft, forward to cut off power to the front-wheel-drive chain sprocket in the 2WD mode or backward to engage full-time 4WD. It also includes a viscous coupling that provides the front-to-rear torque biasing found only on Jeep and AMC four-wheel drive-products."

As indicated, the Jeep Wagoneer essentially is a luxury version of the rough-and-ready military jeeps of World War II and thereafter. It is a bigger vehicle, essentially a compact station wagon, that became one of the most popular off-road candidates after its introduction in 1962. (When it was introduced, to meet the challenge of the luxury-oriented International Harvester Scout, the Jeep line still was being produced by Willys Motors. The next year, Willys was sold to Kaiser Corporation, which renamed the firm Kaiser Jeep. In 1970, the company was sold to American Motors, which is still the producer of models evolved from the original Jeeps and of new versions of the Wagoneer in the 1980s.)

As of the mid-1980s, two basic Jeep models were being built, the CJ-5 and CJ-7, both coming with various body and trim packages. All of these models retained the pure four-wheel-drive transmission system, which made them favorites with off-road racers.

The CJ-5, while featuring many new innovations in design and technology, still bore a close resemblance to the honored MA and MB models of the 1940s. Like those pioneer vehicles, it came in only open or soft body form, while the CJ-7 could be bought with either a soft or a removable hard top. Wheelbase of the CJ-5 is 83.4 inches, almost the same as the 80 inches the U.S. Army originally prescribed for the light reconnaissance cars of the early 1940s that helped spawn the postwar off-road revolution. The maximum overall width of the CJ-5 is about 60 inches compared to 62 for the MA/MB. Overall length is a bit greater—142.9 vs. 132 inches. By comparison, the CJ-7 is considerably larger, with a wheelbase of 93.4 inches and overall length of 153.5 inches as befits a model having more features for ease of conventional paved road operation.

In terms of power, gasoline efficiency, maneuverability and other performance aspects, both the CJ-5 and CJ-7 by the mid-1980s represented several generations of engineering progress. The standard CJ-5 uses a lightweight six-cylinder engine that turns out far more horsepower than the 60-plus of the 1940s models. In terms of miles per gallon, it provided 2 to 3 times the performance of the original model, with a few extra mpg's from the standard four-speed manual transmission over the automatic transmission offered as an option for the CJ-7. (The CJ-7 could be obtained with either a standard four-speed manual trans- or five-speed manual option besides the automatic option.) The CJ-7, but not the CJ-5, also offered an engine option of a four-cyclinder, 2.5 liter engine rather than a six-cylinder power plant.

While U.S. companies like American Motors, Ford, General Motors and Chrysler refined four-wheel-drive designs from the 1960s on, engineers in other nations, particularly Japan, weren't ignoring this technology. Toyota already could point to considerable off-road performance from its redoubtable Land Cruiser series, which was first introduced in the 1950s, and later Datsun and Subaru engineered some notable off-road systems. Subaru made some important contributions to combined two-wheel/four-wheel-drive technology with development of its On Demand 4WD. Among the features long unique to Subaru's four-wheel-drive passenger cars, station wagons and pickup trucks (including its compact Brat mini-truck) are: achievement of full-time front-wheel drive with the primary drivetrain (other 2WD/4WD installations used rear-wheel drive) and a design that permits the driver to shift into four-wheel drive while the vehicle is moving.

The Subaru design approach got underway with the introduction of a standard front-wheel-drive system in its 1969 models. Among the advantages claimed for front-wheel drive are improved handling and traction, plus compactness to maximize interior room. This is achieved partly by avoiding having to place elements of the drivetrain under the passenger or cargo area as is the case with rear-wheel-drive installations. Note that the 1969 system was front-wheel drive, not four-wheel drive.

To optimize this concept, Subaru also decided to match the engine design to the needs of the front-wheel-drive method, a step which also offered advantages for the later four-wheel-drive evolution. As a company engineer put it, "In-line, cast-iron power plants just wouldn't do the job; they work best with rear-wheel drive. Lightweight aluminum alloy is the best material, and a horizontally opposed, four-cylinder layout is the ideal configuration.

"Because these engines are flat rather than tall, they sit low in the engine compartment and yield a lower center of gravity. This results in better handling. Because the pistons move horizontally (that is, parallel to the ground) rather than vertically (up and down), cylinder vibrations tend to cancel each other out to provide lower maintenance and longer engine life. Aluminum engines also heat up and cool down faster for better efficiency."

Using this type of engine also allows designers to come up with car profiles having lower air drag. That is, since the engine sits low, it allows using a front-end profile shaped for good aerodynamic airflow around the vehicle. This minimizes friction between the air molecules and the body surface that causes a resistive force called drag. With lower drag, a vehicle can use less fuel to go a given distance.

The On Demand arrangement in Subaru cars of the 1980s has an inside-the-vehicle selector lever with three positions. Pushed all the way down, the lever moves the four-wheel-drive gears out from the main output shaft to provide front-wheel-drive operation. Moved to the next position, the lever provides for selection of the four-wheel-drive "hi" mode and in the uppermost position, four-wheel-drive "lo." In the latter position, the lever engages the 1.462 reduction gear for 40 percent more pulling torque. Compared to high gear, the gear sets in the four-speed transmission are all lowered proportionately. For example, in first gear, the low range ratio is 5.315 compared to 3.636 for high gear. In operation, when the selector lever is switched to the low range position, it moves a synchronizer sleeve rearward. The action engages a second, separate countergear while disengaging the one used for four-wheel-drive high- and front-wheel drive.

For the high position, the gear ratio between the main shaft gear and the countergear is 1:1. The low range mode is intended for four-wheel-drive operation where extra pulling power is needed for deep snow, sand or off-roading in general. High range permits using four-wheel drive on paved roads.

One of the impressive things about the Subaru four-wheel-drive vehicles of the 1980s was their combination of 4WD capability with surprisingly good fuel efficiency. Under non-off-road conditions, for instance, the model GL wagon had a U.S. Environmental Protection Agency rating of 33 miles per gallon highway and 25 mpg city, as good or better than any four-wheel-drive vehicle available in the United States in the mid-1980s and even better than many new-model conventional two-wheel-drive cars.

In the mid 1980s, the Dual Range, On Demand system was available on Subaru wagons and regular passenger cars such as the GL hatchback. (Both also were produced with four-wheel-drive-only systems.) All of these models typically were powered by an aluminum four-cylinder, liquid-cooled, overhead valve, four-stroke horizontally opposed engine with a compression ratio of 8.7:1. Other specifications: piston displacement, 1,781 cubic centimeters (109 cubic inches); maximum output, 71 brake horsepower at 4,400 revolutions per minute; maximum torque, 94 foot-pounds at 2,400 rpm. The same engine also was used on the open-bed Brat (which is an acronym for Bi-drive Recreational All-terrain Transporter), whose EPA gas mileage ratings of 36 highway and 27 city compared quite well with other mini-trucks offered in the mid-1980s.

Toyota's Land Cruiser, mentioned earlier, first came out in 1958. Patterned somewhat after the Jeep, it proved a formidable contender for off-road use outside the United States and also in time was introduced into the U.S. market as well. The Toyota engineering group didn't come up with any major breakthroughs in 4 × 4 technology during the design's long history, but they did steadily improve the vehicle's reliability and also integrated all of the components of the system to maximize off-road performance.

The experience gained with the Land Cruiser was applied to other Toyota vehicles such as the new 4 × 4 pickup introduced into the United States towards the end of the 1970s. Many U.S. automotive trade press editors dubbed the pickup "the son of Land Cruiser," though they agreed it was "not just a rehash." For instance, editor Tom Madigan of *Off-Road* magazine, which named the design "Four-wheel-drive vehicle of the year" soon after it came out, pointed out the equipment was engineered for true pickup truck operation. "The running gear for the pickup was designed specifically for the truck."

This design, the first of a family of 4 × 4s offered by Toyota in the 1980s, was almost a unanimous choice as four-wheel pickup of the year, winning the same honor from *Off-Road Vehicles* magazine and *PV4* (Pickups, Vans and Four-Wheel Drive) magazine. Dan Brown of *PV4* wrote that the model offered "a very stable design and superior horsepower," enough "to burst out of the apex of a turn . . . and motor up steep hills in second gear . . . It's a vehicle that's in tune with the times; it is light, economical, rugged and dependable, with more than adequate cargo carrying capacity . . . [It] can be driven faster and harder off-road with less chance of damage to undercarriage components."

Madigan echoed that enthusiasm. "Ground clearances were excellent. The truck went everywhere we wanted it to go . . . We found the overall quality of the truck to be outstanding . . . We loved the power steering, the carrying capacity and the gas mileage (typically 21 mpg off-road). The bed was ideal for carrying equipment or even motorcycles."

These comments focus on many of the aspects to be considered in matching any four-wheel-drive vehicle to the user's requirements. And it should be stressed that while this Toyota model won 4×4 vehicle of the year when it first came out, other designs from other manufacturers won honors of that kind in other model years. Since good designs tend to become standards, produced with relatively few basic design changes for a good many years (the aforementioned Land Cruiser wasn't too much different in the 1980s from its forebears in the 1960s), if you put together an honors list covering the current model year and going back 5 or 6 years or so, it would provide a good checklist for choosing a model to suit your current needs.

As of the mid-1980s, Toyota manufactured its half-ton 4WD truck line in standard and long-bed models, the standard bed having a wheel base of 102.2 inches, the long bed 110.6, with overall lengths, respectively, of 171.1 and 186.2 inches. All the models use four-cylinder, single-overhead-cam engines with a displacement of 2,366 cc (2.4 liters), compression ratio of 9:1, power output of 100 hp at 4,800 rpm throughout the United States except in California where air-quality law requirements lowered that to 96 hp at 4,800 rpm. Torque output was 93 foot-pounds at 2,800 rpm. Transmission was a five-speed overdrive system with a differential ratio of 4.10:1.

The Land Cruiser, still keeping changes to a minimum, in the mid-1980s was produced in hardtop and wagon designs, still powered by a six-cylinder, 4.2 liter engine turning out 125 hp at 3,600 rpm. The vehicles have a four-speed manual transmission coupled with a two-speed transfer case. Engine compression ratio is 8.3:1 and torque output 200 foot-pounds at 1,800 rpm.

Also added to the Toyota line in the 1980s was a Tercel

four-wheel-drive station wagon. This features a new six-speed overdrive transmission that includes an extra-low gear for low-speed pulling power in the four-wheel-drive mode. Providing that gear, Toyota noted, permitted elimination of the four-wheel-drive transfer case used in most 4 × 4s. In the two-wheel-drive mode, the transmission functions as a regular five-speed overdrive manual gear box. As in the Subaru passenger car systems noted earlier, the Tercel wagon employs front-wheel drive.

Though Ford Motor Company turned out hundreds of thousands of Jeep-style vehicles during World War II, it didn't concentrate on commercial models as Willys did when the war was over. In fact, at the start of the 1960s, the only two 4 × 4 entries from Ford were the half ton F-100 and three-quarter-ton F-250 pickups available in limited body options. In later years, of course, wider choices of those types were added to the line. In 1966, though, Ford made a major bid for the off-road market with its new Bronco utility vehicles, intended to compete with some of the plusher Jeep and Scout designs.

The Bronco had an up-and-down record for a while, with some versions having only limited appeal to off-roaders. But at the end of the 1960s, design improvements began to give the Bronco a new image, and by the 1970s, Bronco became an important part of Ford's annual sales. The 1978 series, for instance, set a Ford 4 × 4 sales record with a 400 percent gain over the previous year. One of the features of the Bronco in the 1970s and 1980s was its array of powerful engine options. The standard model had a 5.8 liter (351 cubic-inch-displacement) eight-cylinder V-8, or you could select the larger 6.6. liter (400 CID) V-8. With such engines, Bronco offered more payload capacity than many other light trucks. (Its wheelbase of 104 inches and overall length of 180.3 inches are considerably bigger than Jeep, Scout or Land Cruiser models.) It also offered more than 90 options, ranging from seat types for 2 to 6 people, to a padded GT bar, to a swing-away spare tire carrier to an extra-capacity 32-gallon fuel tank.

In the mid 1980s, Ford introduced a smaller Bronco version called the Bronco II. This featured the same twin-traction-beam and independent front suspension and ladder-frame construction of the Big Bronco, but on a 94-inch wheelbase. Instead of an eight-cylinder V-8, the Bronco II uses a V-6 2.8 liter engine rated at 115 hp at 4,600 rpm. By comparison, most other V-6s available in the mid-1980s were rated at 110 hp at 4,800 rpm.

Chrysler Corporation, which built many 4×4 trucks for the military during World War II, stressed larger pickups in its postwar 4×4 activity. Primarily, the line consisted of 114-inch wheelbase half-ton pickups and 122-inch three-quarter-ton models. But a one-ton vehicle also was available. The basic engine design for the models of the 1960s, a slant six, 225 CID power plant, remained the standard for most domestic models in the 1980s. Options included larger engines such as the 318 CID V-8 and the 361 CID V-8.

One model using a different engine is the Dodge Power Ram 50, a small pickup introduced by the company's Dodge Division in the mid-1980s. The 109.4-inch wheelbase vehicle, debuting in 1982, won the 1982 Four Wheeler of the Year award from several publications. At the time, the Ram 50 engine was a compact two-liter four-cylinder unit putting out 90 hp at 5,000 rpm. One of the features of the system is use of an automatic, rather than manual, transmission on standard models.

One of the better known names in 4×4 pickups in the 1970s was the Ramcharger, still a key part of the Dodge family in the 1980s. The standard power plant for the half-ton version is a two-barrel 318 CID teamed with a four-speed manual transmission. Options included automatic transmission and four-barrel engines. (A design essentially the same as the Ramcharger has been produced over the years by Chrysler's Plymouth Division under the "Duster" label.) Among standard Ramcharger features in the 1980s were a 35-gallon fuel tank (giving a potential range of 700 miles without refueling), radial tires and automatic locking hubs on four-wheel-drive models. The hubs lock automatically when the driver shifts into four-wheel drive and are released when the driver shifts out of 4×4 and backs the vehicle up a few feet.

General Motors' Chevrolet Division was offering four-wheel drive on half- and three-quarter-ton pickups at the end of the 1950s, and in the 1960s extended four-wheel drive as an option to almost every model type in small and large trucks. One of the company's first steps into the more general 4×4 market was its Carryall utility model of the early 1960s. The engines for those models ranged from a 230 CID six-cylinder design to a 327 CID V-8.

Still, it took the introduction of the sports/utility Blazer model at the end of the 1960s to make Chevy and GM an important factor with dedicated off-roaders. The Blazer was aimed at the niche occupied by Broncos and Scouts, but with longer wheelbase than the Bronco's 106 inches and greater length. Various engine options from a 292 CID six to 350 CID V-8s were offered during the 1970s and 1980s.

International Harvester's Scout, which played such an important role in the off-road vehicle boom that began in the 1960s, remained pretty much the same as far as basic systems were concerned until the 1970s. At the start of the decade, the Scout II started coming off the line, providing updating throughout the design. Besides having more cargo space, the Scout II had more powerful V-8 engine options as well as power steering, power brakes, air conditioning, and manual or automatic locking front hubs. Unfortunately, as the 1970s went by, the fortunes of this landmark name suffered from the management problems of the parent company that brought International Harvester to the brink of bankruptcy in the early 1980s.

These different models give a broad range of 4×4 designs covering almost any taste or requirement an off-road fan might want. It's by no means a complete list, but the models noted do include the majority of those considered classics of the 1960s and 1970s, as well as those most likely to gain that ranking in the 1990s and beyond.

Among the models rated in the top ten "collectibles" for the 1970s by John Gunnell in his *Complete Four Wheel Drive Manual* are: the International Harvester Scout II Travel Top, American Motors/Hurst customized 1971 Jeepster, Ford 1971 Baja Bronco, American Motors 1973 Jeep pickup, Chevrolet 1973 Blazer Hardtop, Plymouth 1974 Duster Hardtop, Dodge 1974 Ramcharger 440 Hardtop, American

Motors 1977 Jeep Honcho, Subaru 1977 4×4 station wagon, Subaru 1978 Brat mini-truck, American Motors 1980 Eagle.

Because of their ruggedness and reliability, off-road vehicles tend to have a long life. Off-road fans often seek out and lovingly care for models not only from recent decades, but ones going back to the Jeeps of World War II. In addition, manufacturers who come up with classic designs tend to stick with a winner and many of the new 4×4s turned out in the 1980s, as we've indicated, are essentially the same as their predecessors. So too, many of the 1980s models may still be running or even coming off production lines in the next decade and perhaps beyond.

3
PICKING AN OFF-ROAD CYCLE

Like 4 × 4s, off-road motorcycling has drawn the interest of millions of people since World War II, with the most dramatic growth in off-road racing and recreational activities coming in the 1970s and 1980s. It is estimated that in the United States today over 10 million people own motorcycles and about one fifth to one quarter of those are off-road models.

Fans of both 4 × 4s and off-road cycles tend to be individualists, but perhaps those who ride cycles are a little more so. Stu Munro, who developed impressive training courses for novice cyclists in Canada talked about that. "Riding a motorcycle is not necessarily dangerous, but there is an element of danger involved. It follows that a motorcyclist is an adventurous person. Not only that, but a youngster who buys a bike is someone who wants to be independent. He doesn't want to rely on other people for lifts. He wants to go when and where the spirit takes him."

Motorcycling is also a relatively inexpensive and unregimented way to go, particularly for off-road activities. A typical street bike or combination (a bike designed for use on both street and dirt) has to be registered with your state's department of motor vehicles, but a bike used purely for off-road presently doesn't have to be registered.

At this writing, states generally don't require liability insurance for off-road motorcycle operation, although it would be a good idea to check with the Motor Vehicle Department in your area to make sure there haven't been any recent changes in state regulations. However, if you plan to use a motorcycle on the street, the situation changes. The rule of thumb is, the minute you put the front wheel on pavement, you'd better have insurance. While you don't need insurance for dirt operation only, if available, it might be worthwhile for theft and damage protection.

Partly because of the excitement of off-roading, partly because an off-road cycle can permit a rider to go many places inaccessible to bigger 4×4 vehicles (sometimes even inaccessible to horses), and partly because of economics, off-road sales have been increasing at a greater rate than other types of motorcycle models in recent years. Off-road motorcycle racer Jim Rice of Palo Alto, California, recalled that pricing played a big role when he bought his first cycle. "I just couldn't afford to buy a car and pay for its insurance. So I bought a bike and insured it and still had enough money to live on."

Once he got out in the back country, he found he preferred off-road cycling to any other form. "I'd rather ride off the road. There aren't as many unexpected things popping up in your path when you're puttering through the woods, or exploring some rugged old wasteland."

Of course, that's an oversimplification. You don't have to worry about a car going through a red light or stop sign or unexpectedly changing lanes on a crowded freeway. But there are natural things to contend with that don't trouble a rider on pavement—unexpected ruts or mudholes, low-hanging branches, rocks or sticks. Off-road riders have to be self-sufficient, able to improvise "fixes" for equipment failures off the beaten path and careful about having the right equipment that's correctly maintained.

One thing off-road motorcyclists don't have to be concerned with is four-wheel drive. The majority of off-road cycles used today have only two wheels and the driving force comes from only one of those. But even for three-wheelers or the occasional four-wheel motorcycle, the vehicles are so compact and the wheels so close together that the effects we've discussed for 4×4s have minimal impact even if an off-road bike is driven on paved road.

Which doesn't mean there aren't different design requirements for a dirt bike as compared to a street bike. And, of course, there also are differences between dirt bikes intended for recreational use and those intended for motocross and other types of off-road racing. Besides that, there also can be subtle variations between off-road bikes designed for desert-type terrain, such as is found in the western United States, and the grass-and-woods setting elsewhere.

Those differences extend to things like tire design, type of engine, engine cooling techniques, suspension system and even handlebars. On an off-road bike intended mainly for back-country use it's better to have narrower handlebars than for an equivalent pavement or motocross cycle. These handlebars make it easier to maneuver between trees or narrow passages. It's generally better too for these handlebars to be tilted back more than for street use. You don't have to worry about tree-hemmed paths for typical motocross cycling, but handlebar design does differ somewhat from other type bikes for better handling under racing conditions.

In terms of engines, it's generally desirable to have a more rugged design for off-road operation than for street use. This has to be coupled with good flexibility in the way the power is applied to the wheels. Thus a good off-road cycle generally employs a gear system allowing a wider range of gear ratios than a street system. Since an off-road engine often has to work harder to move a motorcycle through and over unprepared paths, mudholes, sand, than a similar sized pavement unit, it needs more cooling capability to get rid of excess heat generated under those environments. Engine cooling can be achieved passively, by having a large amount of metal surface from which engine heat is conducted into the air, or actively through things like water circulation. Almost all automobiles, of course, use the latter technique with water pumped around engine sections to pick up heat which then is passed into the air through the radiator.

Until recently, close to 100 percent of motorcycles used passive cooling. If you look at the engine installation on those bikes, you can see the arrays of thin metal sections sticking out from the cylinder head. Heat from the engine goes into the cylinder walls, then moves into that series of fins for dissipation into the atmosphere. Since the amount of cooling is related to the total metal surface in contact with the outside air, you can get more cooling by increasing the number of fins or by increasing their width. If you put passively cooled street bikes and off-road bikes of the same horsepower class together, you can see that the fin area is larger for the off-road system.

In recent years, some motorcycle manufacturers have begun to offer water-cooled designs. Water cooling can do more effective cooling than a passive system, but it obviously increases the complexity of the system through the need for extra parts and a water pump that isn't required for a passively cooled system.

Still, the steady advances in motorcycle technology have brought practical water-cooled engines to the fore. For backcountry riding an active cooling system has the drawback of giving the bike something else that could go wrong. For instance, while you could get a leak in a water circulating radiator, nothing much is likely to happen to metal fins. Even if one or two fins broke off, which is highly unlikely, the cooling effect would be pretty well handled by the remaining fins. It should be emphasized, though, that current water-cooled equipment has been made highly reliable so that failures are kept to a minimum.

For some applications, particularly racing, where an active system can give a competitive edge, it's well worth considering. So while many dirt or trail bikes for recreational use don't use water cooling, more and more competition models go that route. For instance, Honda's CR125R and CR250R motocross models and the heavy-duty XR500R design (where the numbers refer to the piston displacements in cubic centimeters) feature it. Describing how their system works, Honda reports, "A gear-driven pump circulates the water which flows into the cylinder, cylinder head, through the twin interconnected aluminum radiators where it cools and then flows back into the pump."

Advantages of such cooling, Honda points out, are that "it allows higher and more consistent power output, increased engine longevity and easier maintenance. Since cylinder cooling and expansion rates are so accurately controlled, a reborable steel liner is used in these engines. [i.e., the original cylinder housing can be reworked rather than having to install new liners]."

A major consideration is what kind of engine works best for specific applications. Obviously, with the many bike models on the market, engine performance for different designs varies all over the place, but almost all motorcycle power plants fall into two broad groupings, two-stroke or four-stroke, also known as two-cycle or four-cycle. What that means is that in a two-stroke engine the piston goes up and down twice for one fuel-air mixture explosion and in a four-stroke system it goes up and down four times for one such explosion.

In a two-stroke design the piston moves down once and then back up. Typically, as the piston moves upward, the bottom surface uncovers an opening, or intake port, in the cylinder wall and, at the same time, its upper surface closes an opening called a transfer port. The lower entrance to the transfer port is roughly opposite the intake port at the bottom of the cylinder housing. The upper opening is placed about halfway up the cylinder wall. The upward action of the piston creates a vacuum beneath it that causes a supply of fresh fuel-air mixture from the carburetor to come into that section and move towards the transfer port. Meanwhile, there already is a charge of fuel and air in the top of the cylinder being forced into a steadily smaller volume by the piston.

When the piston is as high as it's allowed to go, a spark plug whose bottom end extends into the upper cylinder area is activated by a flow of electric current so that a spark is generated through a small gap in the metal ends of the plug. That spark causes the fuel-air mixture to start burning, causing the explosion that forces the piston down on the second, or power stroke. That motion of the piston causes the crankshaft attached to it to rotate and this power output is then sent through the gear system to turn the rear wheel.

As the piston moves down, its top part uncovers the exhaust port first, then the transfer port. During this step, the bottom of the piston forces the new fuel-air mixture into the bottom end of the transfer port and the mixture rushes upward into the top part of the cylinder. As it does, it helps sweep the used-up combustion products from the earlier explosion out through the exhaust port. After the piston reaches the bottom of its travel, it is ready to move up to start the process all over. (It's the rotating action of the crankshaft that provides the energy to move the piston back up.)

A variation of the two-stroke method, called the rotary-valve two-stroke cycle, is used by some manufacturers. In this system, intake of the fuel mixture from the carburetor is controlled by a metal disk attached to the crankshaft rather than by the piston surface. A small section of the disk is cut away so that it opens the passage from the carburetor to the cylinder at the right time in the cycle. Companies employing this design in some of their engines include Kawasaki and Yamaha.

The cylinders used in four-stroke cycle engines don't have ports in the cylinder walls. Instead, the fuel mixture is injected and the burned gases removed by means of small valves usually located in the top portion, or cylinder head. The valves are opened or closed at the correct moment in the cycle by small, specially shaped parts called cams. The cams, in turn, are fastened to a rotating arm known as a camshaft. For an engine with more than one cylinder, there will be several sets of cams on the camshaft, with their positions slightly varied so that the valves of the different cylinders open in a desired sequence to keep the power output, and thus the crankshaft movement, running smoothly.

Some engines have the camshaft located in the crankcase, but most modern motorcycle engines have it placed just above the cylinder heads. The latter are called overhead cam engines. The system can be designed so one cam can operate both valves; this is done by shaping the cam so it meets with different linkages for the valves at different points in its path. Such a system is referred to as a single overhead cam design (SOHC). Or there can be two cams, one to operate intake and one to run exhaust valves in the double overhead (also called dual overhead) system (DOHC). Typically, the single cam design is used for smaller-sized motorcycles, and the double cam system can be found in most medium-sized and large bikes.

Although we're emphasizing motorcycles here, the basic engine principles apply for just about all automobiles. However, the standard cycle used in four-wheelers is the four-stroke one. Of course, since automobile engines must turn out more horsepower to move the bigger vehicle and payload weight, these engines are larger and heavier. They obviously will have larger piston systems and will usually burn higher-energy fuel-air mixtures to increase the driving force transmitted to the wheels. There was a time when automobile engines used many more cylinders per engine than bikes, cars having systems with four, six or eight cylinders and most cycles having just one. In recent years, though, the trend in cycle design is toward two- and four-cylinder systems (referred to as V-twins, transverse fours, etc.).

In any case, whether for a motorcycle or an automobile, the four-stroke cycle begins with the intake stroke during which the piston is moving downward and the cam causes the intake valve to open while the exhaust valve is closed. During this phase, the downward motion of the piston causes the pressure above it to decrease, causing a suction effect to draw a charge of fuel and air in through the intake valve. When the piston reaches the lowest point in its travel, the rotation of the cam causes the intake valve to close. Now the crankshaft makes the piston rise again on the second stroke. With both valves closed to prevent the fuel from escaping, the top of the piston drives that mixture into a smaller and smaller volume. Since the piston on this stroke is compressing the fuel and air, it is called the compression stroke.

When the piston has reached the top of its travel, an electric spark is triggered by the distributor system. The spark shoots across the spark-plug gap to ignite the fuel-air mixture. As the gases burn and expand, they force the piston back down for a second time in the power stroke. It is this energy which goes from crankshaft through the transmission to the wheels but, as we've seen before, some of the energy from the power stroke serves to keep the crankshaft moving the pistons up and down. When the second down stroke is completed, the piston is ready for the fourth stroke—the second upward stroke in the four-stroke cycle—the exhaust stroke. In this final part of the four-stroke cycle, the piston moves upward, pushing the exhaust gases out through the now opened exhaust valve. At the top of this stroke, the exhaust valve is closed by the cam system, the intake valve is opened and the cycle is ready to start again.

The two-stroke engine is simpler than the four-stroke, since it has fewer moving parts, doesn't require a separate oil pump and doesn't call for careful adjustment of things like the camshaft-valve system. In general, a two-stroke engine is less expensive than a four-stroke one. But the four-stroke has plenty of features in its favor. For one, its valve system, if properly designed, gives closer control over the amount of fuel-air mixture injected on each cycle which can give better fuel efficiency. It also runs more smoothly than the two-stroke system over a greater range of engine speeds and is less likely to stall out during idling.

Until recently, the simplicity of a good two-stroke engine led most cycle experts to prefer it for off-road operations. The two-stroke design also had a considerable development lead over four-stroke systems, because the emphasis for several decades after World War II was on two-stroke power plants. However, as the desire among designers and potential users for higher performance became greater, cycle manufacturers, Honda in particular, put more and more effort into four-stroke concepts. By the end of the 1970s, the four-stroke design had become increasingly sophisticated, to the point where reliable, rugged, high-performance engines were available for off-road as well as pavement bikes.

Thus most of Honda's dual-purpose and dirt-bike models in the early 1980s used four-stroke engines. Enduro types like the XR200R (195 cc), XR250R (249 cc) and XR500R (498 cc) used four-stroke single-vertical-cylinder engines. All of Honda's dual-purpose bikes from the smallest, the CT70 (72 cc) minibike, to the largest, the 498 cc XL500R, were built with four-stroke engines, although some of them had other than a single-vertical-cylinder arrangement. Actually, the larger dual-purpose bikes and the Enduros were essentially the same as far as engines and drivetrain, but the suspension and brake systems were built differently, to match off-road performance for dirt and trail use in the case of dual purpose, and Enduro competition in the other.

The ability of a four-stroke, water-cooled, medium-sized bike to cope with the most demanding off-road terrain was demonstrated by the performance of a special Honda XR500R model in the 1982 Baja 1000 race in Mexico. That cycle, a specially prepared version ridden by the team of Al Baker and Jack Johnson, not only won the race, but finished so far ahead of its nearest competitor that Baker, who had brought it across the finish line, was already back at his hotel and asleep by the time the next cycle completed the course.

This exceptional win was achieved despite an unexpected collision between Baker's cycle and a cow that briefly knocked Baker unconscious and confused him so that he went the wrong way for a while. As he recalled in *Cycle* magazine (March 1983), "After I crashed into the cow, the bike stalled and the lights went out. It was pitch black and I was disoriented. (This happened at night.) When I finally found the bike and got it started, I had no idea which direction was La Paz. So I just started down the road. After four or five miles I came to a truck I thought I'd passed before. There was a guy sitting inside waiting for the racers to go by. So I pulled up and asked, '¿Donde esta La Paz?' He pointed down the road in the direction I had just come. I had been riding backward on the course. I turned around, gassed it up and 25 miles later hit La Paz." (Total time for Baker and Johnson from Ensenada to La Paz: 17 hours, 25 minutes.)

That accomplishment in its origins also reflected the cross-pollination between off-road racing and motorcycle design. Baker, after arranging to set up the U.S. distributorship for the Japanese firm of Mugen in the late 1970s (Mugen Japan is headed by Hirotoshi Honda, son of Honda founder Soichiro Honda), became interested in an arrangement with Honda research for modifying experimental models for improved off-road racing performance. As part of this program, in the early 1980s he got the chance to work with early versions of the XR500R. The one sent him in early 1982 had all the key features planned for the commercial version, though not necessarily in final, optimized form. Among these were a full-cradle, chrome-molybdenum frame using "Pro-Link" rear suspension and a special dry-sump Radial Four-Valve Combustion Chamber. As the name indicates, the valves are located at an angle to the cylinder housing center line, rather than in the conventional vertical position. This changed valve position had been used successfully in cars Honda had built for Formula II auto racing. It allowed the internal shape of the cylinder to be designed for much more efficient combustion of the fuel-air mixture.

Features like that still had to be tested in actual operation to make sure they worked properly under motorcycle environments. Baker and his associates ran tests and did pre-runs over off-road courses. From that, his company came up with suggestions for improvements and also outlined problems they felt needed to be solved. The Honda team in Japan went to work on those inputs and introduced the resulting fixes or modifications into several more XR500Rs that were shipped to Baker in the summer of 1982. The new bikes were used in several off-road races and subjected to shop testing and examination for still better honing of the design's capability. Finally, in the fall, all of that expertise was applied to the final version that Baker and Johnson rode to victory. In 1983, the first stock XR500Rs were delivered to U.S. dealers for showroom display, production models almost identical to the one that conquered the Baja.

The promise of the four-stroke engine wasn't lost on other companies in the field. By the time the XR500R was cruising down the Baja, most major manufacturers had extensive four-stroke model lines in the market. For example, Suzuki employed that type engine on its SP125Z (124 cc) and SP250Z (249 cc) dual purpose trail/street/sport models and on the DR125 and DR250 off-road/sport designs. Suzuki in its larger bikes typically used four valves per cylinder rather than two, an approach also taken by Honda in its higher-powered models.

In the four-valve system, each cylinder head is fitted with two intake and two exhaust valves, with each of these valves somewhat smaller than their counterparts in the conventional two-valve design. Obviously, this adds some complexity, since more valves are involved and the cam system must be held to even closer tolerances to insure that each pair opens and closes together. But, on the other hand, this improves system performance for many types of operation.

Honda engineers point out that one thing this allows is a central spark plug location "for stable combustion at high rpm, even at high compression ratios. By using four smaller valves instead of two larger ones, more overall port area and better 'breathing' can be obtained. Individual valve weight can also be reduced. Reducing valve weight, especially for larger intake valve weight, means that higher rpm levels can be achieved before valve 'float' occurs. This is especially important for DOHC engines as it allows valve adjustment shims to be located on top of the valve caps for easy maintenance without the risk of shim dislodgment from valve float at high rpm. Compared to some other designs, Honda four-valve DOHC systems can be maintained without having to remove the camshafts and, as the valve pairs are very close together, two valves can be checked or adjusted simultaneously, further reducing maintenance time."

All of which doesn't mean that two-stroke designs have disappeared. There were plenty of efficient, smoothly operating two-stroke dirt bikes on the market in the 1980s in just about all size classes. This group includes Yamaha models, such as the YZ250K and such European contenders as the Maico 250-cc Spider from Germany and the Husky XC500 from Sweden's Husqvarna Corporation. Two-stroke designs tended to be more popular in the small cycle/minibike class, a good example being Kawasaki's KX80E, considered one of the best performing types in its class after it appeared on the market in improved form over earlier Kawasaki 80-cc models in 1983. (As one test rider enthused after riding a demonstration model in 1983, "The latest green 80 is a missile!") Reflecting technology trends in the '80s, while earlier 80-cc Kawasaki cycles had used passive cooling, the new KX80E went to water cooling.

Though we've devoted most of this chapter to a discussion of engines, since no vehicle can be much better than its prime mover, a good motorcycle design must include attention to every system feature from tires and suspension to the transmission. In the transmission area, a good selection of gear ratios and well meshed gear operation naturally is a key factor and has received much design study over the years. In the 1980s, the drive system, which had remained relatively static in terms of design innovations for some time, came in for more scrutiny, particularly from the U.S.-based cycle builder, Harley Davidson.

In the mid-1980s, Harley began building some of its models with belt drive rather than shafts or chains. As its engineers pointed out, belts were nothing new. Early motorcycles had used them to get power from transmission to wheels. However, steel belts tended to be heavy and less efficient than other devices, such as drive chains, so that had fallen by the wayside. But advances in high-strength materials, they noted, offered ways to design long-life, lightweight belts. In Harley Davidson's case, plastic composite materials using aramid fiber offered very flexible belts with strengths that matched those of steel. Harley Davidson's claims for its new system included lower weight and simpler design than a shaft, resulting in less power loss. A company brochure stated, "Compared to a chain, it's smoother shifting, quieter, requires no lubrication and needs minimal adjustment. It will last up to three times longer than a chain and in case of emergency there's an accessory belt that can be installed in fifteen minutes."

At the time, Harley was bucking the general design trend, though it often happens that the unusual design becomes the normally accepted one after a time. Another firm bucking the trend in the mid-1980s was Husqvarna, which built bikes with twin shock absorbers rather than the single-shock systems favored by all the other major cycle producers. The general feeling was that single shocks could be designed to take off-road impacts more readily without the imbalance that could take place with two separate units. Husqvarna, however, devised special damping systems sensitive to both speed and position that company engineers believed would actually give a more comfortable ride under off-road conditions.

Though there was considerable skepticism from other

companies in the field about this, the Husky XC500 seemed to satisfy more than a few of the critics. After a test ride, Tom Webb of *Dirt Bike* magazine reported, "This is a Husky that you can trail ride, motocross, hare scramble, or race desert, with hardly a mod needed. If only it were ten pounds lighter [dry weight without gas was 247.5 lb] it might just be perfect. Even so, the XC is a great bike for the guy who wants something powerful, that handles, and is just plain fun."

Whether you're talking about a brute force 4×4 large pickup or a minicycle, having the right tires is always a prime concern. It often happens that this calls for replacing the standard ones that come with a new bike with other types that give better performance. This suggestion often crops up in test riders' reports on new models that perform quite well in other respects. After making very enthusiastic comments about the Yamaha YZ250 1983 model, for instance, *Dirt Bike* staffers stated, "Take off that annoying front Bridgestone knobbette and put on a real tire if you want the YZ to turn properly. Try a Metzeler." Similarly, Metzelers were recommended in place of the Pirelli Sandcross tires used on initial production models of the Maico 250-cc Spider.

Besides the items mentioned, there are numerous other component add-ons or replacements you can look into if you have the time, money and desire to upgrade your cycle. There are dozens of companies making all kinds of lighting systems, fairings, rear-view mirrors and other accessories. Magazines like *Cycle Guide, Cycle, Dirt Bike, Motorcycling* and similar publications often have special issues cataloging most or all of the products available along with costs and manufacturers.

In the same way, these publications have special editions dealing with major system elements from tires to complete bikes. While this is a field where changes take place all the time with most manufacturers coming out with new models every year, a close look would show that many of these really are old reliables with some new "window dressing." Nevertheless, you will still want to consult annual directory issues to get some idea of what's available when you're in the market for a bike.

One general point worth emphasizing: for best off-road performance you need an off-road-only bike. Dual-purpose models for operation on both pavement and dirt represent a compromise. The difficulty with an off-road-only model, of course, is that you need some way to transport it from urban areas to the back country. Some lucky families solve this by having a 4 × 4 pickup to haul their dirt bikes to the premium spots of off-roading.

4
DO'S AND DON'TS OF OFF-ROADING

Even if you've never been in the back country with a biking or a four-wheel-drive group, you would probably guess that the requirements, and many of the driving considerations, are different from street or highway travel. While you can be almost any age to learn to ride a motorcycle, you usually have to be sixteen or older to get behind the wheel of a four-wheel-drive vehicle. But by getting some insight into what's involved in off-road driving now, you can be ready for the time when you can handle a four-wheel vehicle yourself, and pass along some worthwhile suggestions about off-road activities to friends or family at the same time.

Obviously the details of back-country operation vary considerably when one compares a relatively small, compact motorbike to a large four-wheel vehicle, but many of the general do's and don'ts apply across the board. For instance, it's true that before any off-road trip every vehicle should be carefully inspected to ensure that things are in first-rate condition—that the tires are properly inflated and have no flat spots or excessive wear; that the motor is working well and the oil level is correct; that key parts are clean and in good order. Whether for a motorcycle or a four-wheeler, it's a good idea to have a written checklist you can go over before you begin any back-road journey.

Of course, being familiar with the parts of a vehicle and how things work is particularly valuable. This knowledge isn't vital for conventional paved road operation where, if something goes wrong, there are usually plenty of other people and vehicles around or a nearby phone to call for help. But when something goes wrong on the off roads, if the driver or someone else in the party isn't able to figure out the problem and the remedy, the result is a long, possibly dangerous, walk back through rough terrain. So it makes good sense to study the owner's manual for the particular bike or four-wheeler that's being used. Most motorcycle manufacturers give buyers detailed manuals showing exploded views for assembling various major subsystems with parts lists for each. An exploded view is a diagram in which the different items, such as nuts, bolts and rods, making up a system are shown in a spread-out fashion. Typically, automotive companies may not supply much literature, but detailed manuals for major vehicle makes usually can be bought in automotive parts stores or book stores.

One of the nice things about the motorcycle field, particularly since the advent of small cycles or minibikes, is that someone interested in riding can start learning the basics even in pre-teen years. You don't even have to own your own two-wheeler. There are a lot of courses given by various youth organizations, including the YMCA and YWCA, and under the auspices of bike manufacturers, where the training cycles are provided for students needing them. In these courses, students learn the principles of the motorcycle, what to look for to make sure everything's tip-top before starting to ride, and finally solo, unrestricted riding. For more experience, in many areas and programs riders can proceed to places set aside by cities, counties or states for recreational riding or to privately owned minibike or motorcycle parks.

As this suggests, motorcycle beginners typically spend a lot of their learning time off-road. For one thing, there aren't the licensing restrictions of pavement operation. Yamaha officials stress, "Dirt riding may actually be the best way to start out in motorcycling. There's no automobile traffic to contend with and you can choose your own reasonable speed. Most important, you'll learn to control your machine by leaning and shifting your weight."

Such changes in body position represent one major difference between bike riding and automotive driving. But the philosophy involved in off-road operation is in many ways the same for bikes and four-wheelers. For either vehicle, a good operator realizes he or she generally must drive more slowly and exercise greater patience on dirt than on pavement.

Many of the points made by Datsun in its recommendations for four-wheel-drive off-road driving could be paraphrased for motorcycle riding.

"When you drive off-pavement, the first thing you need to do is slow down. Get used to letting things happen at a more leisurely pace. Don't worry about driving too slowly. [However, for either car or bike, you naturally must maintain sufficient speed, even if low, to keep moving ahead. It's important, though, to be ready to stop and carefully consider how to cope with difficult obstacles.]

"As you gain experience, you'll find that you become more sensitive to the traction conditions of the road or trail you're on. You'll find yourself beginning to make deductions and filling in the blanks. Has another vehicle been through here or is yours the first since the last rains? On an up-slope, you may notice a place where another driver has lost traction and spun his wheels. That tells you something. Coming to a stream crossing, you'll automatically look for tracks on the other side. That's called being trail-smart."

Whether on a bike or in an automobile, the operator must constantly be looking ahead for obstacles—bumps, potholes, logs or even an animal darting across the trail.

In notes prepared for a Datsun-sponsored 4WD off-road driving course, the company stated, "Remember that being an expert off-pavement operator is something of an art. It doesn't mean assaulting every obstacle with brute force. It means figuring out what needs to be done and then doing it with the minimum of crash, bash and smash. Do it with finesse, that's called class."

Another point that applies generally to all types of vehicles is the method of taking an uphill grade. The maxim is not to take it at an angle if at all possible, unless there's no other way or there's a trail or road that has been used by other vehicles. It's also a universal truism that you shouldn't stop on the way up a slope if you can avoid it. Also, for a loose surface, whether in a car or on a bike, it's advisable to start accelerating before you begin the upward movement—not too fast so you can't maintain complete control, but quickly enough to provide momentum.

For going uphill, and indeed, for off-road motorcycle riding in general, you have to know how to ride standing up on the foot pegs, an action naturally not required in automobiles. Yamaha experts point out, "In this position, the legs act as shock absorbers, smoothing out bumps and jolts. Up on the pegs you can shift your weight back and forth with ease. This allows you to control traction and direction over rugged and loose surfaces." The rule is, for an uphill grade, lean forward to move the bike's center of gravity to a more balanced position. Conversely, on the downhill slope you should lean backward to put more weight on the rear wheel to keep the bike from tipping forward.

Whether in an automobile or on a bike, braking is an important factor when going up or down hills. Going uphill the front brake is relied on to provide a lot of extra force to oppose the bike's tendency to slide back down if you come to a stop. But on a downhill run, you must remember the front brake has to be applied very carefully. If you apply too much front brake all at once, your bike can go out of control or pitch over. Instead of using the front brake on a downhill slope, your best approach is to shift to second gear and allow the compression effects of the engine to provide braking power. You supplement this with a light touch on your rear brake. (The front brake usually is controlled by a lever on the handlebars, while the rear one is controlled by a foot pedal.)

For most cycle riding over dirt surfaces, good operation depends on gaining a feel for what's needed in riding position on the pegs and for the right gear and throttle touch. The best approach is to get that insight right from the start, either from a good instruction course or a highly experienced rider, then test it out on some close-to-home dirt surfaces and gradually work up to more difficult and more remote terrain.

For cycling in sand, particularly deep sand, the general rule is to stand up on the foot pegs and transfer your weight as far to the rear as possible. At the same time, you should pull up on the front wheel so that it skims the surface and won't dig in. An experienced instructor also emphasizes, "Once under way, use the highest gear possible. That doesn't mean the very top gear on the bike, but the highest you can go and still keep moving ahead. If you get in too high a gear, you will notice the machine will begin to lose power. When you sense that, downshift a gear while maintaining power."

For practicing off-road skills, Honda outlines a number of different course layouts which can be set up by positioning a series of plastic markers (which could consist of discarded plastic containers or, if available, hay bales). These include an egg-shaped, oval course where one person can stand in the middle and observe the rider's posture and shifting technique; a figure-eight course for practicing left and right turns; a "weaving" arrangement to gain experience on traversing a curving route; and a slalom or "snake" course for testing ability on tight turns. Another layout has markers on either side of a straight course where the rider practices control by trying to steer down the center as slowly as possible while keeping his or her feet on the pegs.

The prime goal of such practice is to develop all the skills of steering, shifting, etc., to the point that you can do them almost automatically. Honda instructors stress, "For good off-road riding, you really need to operate your bike by feel, not having to look down for gear shift or brake levers. You should go on your way with knees pressed against the gas tank, feet on the pegs and eyes pointed ahead, part of the machine."

In this way, you're always using your eyes to look where you're going, to scout for potential hazards. (That kind of concentration is important for automobile driving too.) When you see hazards, your reflexes must take over and make any gear, brake or throttle changes needed for the particular maneuver.

This includes having your legs always ready to stand up on the pegs if a bump is coming up or you're going to ride up a hill. We noted it's important to stand up on the pegs for many parts of back-country riding, but that doesn't mean all the time. Obviously, for extended back-country travel you'd get tired in the upright or semi-upright position all the time. But you have to sense when standing on the pegs what reaction is called for and do it almost without thinking about it.

Knowing what to do if a motorcycle has to be stopped or if the engine stalls on you is important whether you're riding on pavement or off-road. But there are more unexpected hazards to take into consideration off-road. For this reason, the rule is for the rider to keep his or her feet on the pegs until the bike is completely stopped. Otherwise, your foot could come down in a hole or rut or in the path of a rock, which could lead to serious injury, particularly undesirable in lonely places. The front brake lever has to be pulled up sharply in the final phase of stopping and you must school yourself to always get off on the uphill side of the bike so that if it falls over you won't find yourself under it.

Motorcycle riding always calls for wearing protective clothing, whether the trip is made on pavement or dirt, whereas that's not a "must" for most recreational automobile travel. (Of course, going into the back country in an open four-wheeler is another matter, and obviously you'd wear warm clothing if you expected to go outside under severe weather conditions.) However, a cyclist needs considerably more extensive and rugged clothing for back-country excursions as compared to street riding.

The minimum equipment most manufacturers and cycle experts recommend for street operation consists of a good helmet, eye protection, sweat shirt with long sleeves, gloves, long pants (preferably of corduroy or denim material), and heavy leather shoes. For off-road cycling, it's suggested that, instead of heavy shoes, boots be worn, and the higher the boot the better for more protection. Laced boots are preferred for helping to prevent sprained ankles. Also, besides a sweat shirt, a rider should wear a heavy vinyl or heavy leather jacket. The pants also should preferably be made of vinyl or heavy leather. A Honda riding manual warns further, "Flared pants can catch on things such as the kick starter and are not recommended; straight-cut pants without cuff should be used."

It's generally advisable for a cyclist to have a good selection of tools and spares for emergency repairs, and this is particularly vital for off-roaders. A starting point obviously is the tool kit a manufacturer provides with each model. Typically this includes several open end wrenches, a box wrench or two, various regular and Phillips (cross-head) screwdrivers, and a spark-plug wrench. Good additions for off-road trips are a 6-to-8-inch vise-grip wrench and long-nose pliers with a wire-cutter provision. Among the things a rider should add are a tire-repair kit and some kind of tire-inflation device. A good, compact selection of key spare parts also is needed, including extra spark plugs, nuts and bolts, etc. If you're involved in outfitting a motorcycle for off-road use, it's a good idea to talk to someone with a lot of back-country experience to develop the right list of spares for your needs.

And no one should go out in the wilds alone. As in many other activities, such as hiking or snorkeling, the buddy system is in order. For any trip away from "civilization," having a buddy along to give emergency aid or to go for help is only common sense.

The same thing applies to four-wheel-drive vehicles. A car or pickup may seem much bigger than a motorcycle and more rugged, but if things go wrong in the back country, it's just as important to have one or more buddies along to lend a helping hand.

Just as an experienced biker will have a spares kit, a four-wheel enthusiast will make sure there's a carefully chosen selection of spares, repair equipment and survival gear on board. One of the important items is a good tire pump, since back road travel calls for a number of changes in tire pressure for proper operation under different conditions. Along with that go such things as tire irons, tire valve cores and a tool to remove them, rim sealant, tire repair kits, tire gauge and at least two spare tires and wheels (plus spare tubes if the vehicle doesn't have tubeless tires), plus a spare jack.

And that's just the beginning. As you might expect, a good selection of screwdrivers, wrenches, pliers, hacksaws, hammer, fasteners, tape (including black plastic tape and plumbing and heating tape) are important. Then you'll want to include articles like battery jumper cables, electrical wire, spare hoses and belts, extra spark plugs, tow chains or ropes, tire chains, sand mats, an axe, shovel, flares, rags, work gloves, fire extinguisher, flashlights and fuses. Besides those, extra brake fluid, engine oil, gas cans and various leak repair substances can come in handy. Finally, it's usually a good idea to have containers of water both for the vehicle and for drinking, emergency food rations, a pocket compass, emergency blankets, and matches in a waterproof case.

Even though taking such precautions, it's obviously best to plan trips to minimize emergency situations. Most four-wheel-drive experts don't recommend that non-professional operators go to extremes in making use of the capabilities of off-road vehicles. A member of American Motors' Jeep design team warns, "As you leave the pavement behind, you should be guided by the principle that although your 4WD vehicle might be able to go almost any place, there are places you shouldn't go. Use common sense and remember that driving situations and conditions change quickly out there, so be alert and prepared. As a general rule, you should go where others have gone before. There are plenty of 4WD trails or unimproved roads to take you to the great outdoors. Of course, those are unpaved and call for different driving methods than for paved roads."

You should always keep in mind the need to check out a number of things right when you're moving from a paved to an unpaved road. These include deciding the right setting for the transmission control lever and, if the vehicle is one requiring manual setting of the hubs, that they are in locked position. Tire pressure also has to be adjusted. The consensus is that before moving on to an unpaved road, the tire pressure should be reduced to about 2/3 the normal paved road level. And, conversely, these things should be readjusted when going back from off-road to pavement.

Assuming it's a dry sand or dirt road, the driver must remember that the shoulders and curves may be loose or soft, while the crown of the trail may be hard. AMC Jeep in its 4WD driving recommendations states, "Ideally you should have all four wheels on the solid surface, so drive as high up on the crown as possible while staying on your side of the road. You may want to drive in third gear (or in second range if you have automatic transmission) and you should proceed cautiously and slowly, avoiding abrupt steering changes. Also be alert for rutted or choppy road surface, especially the kind of surface that might cause your vehicle's wheels to leave the ground. As a general rule, on pavement or off, keep your vehicle in a situation where at least three wheels are on the surface at all times."

The advantage to using lower pressure in 4 × 4 tires for off-road runs is that this gives better traction and a more comfortable ride. The pressure should never be so low that it might cause separation of tire from rim or failure of a valve stem. On the other hand, if a vehicle is going to be driven at relatively high off-road speeds, a tire pressure closer to paved levels would minimize possible damage from rocks or debris. However, unless someone is involved in the Baja 1000 or some other racing event, slow but sure is the rule anyway. Even speeds as low as five to ten miles per hour are preferable for rugged terrain.

Most 4 × 4s offer the driver selection of gearing for low range or high range. These terms refer to the availability of a range of settings for low-speed or high-speed operation. Experienced off-roaders not involved in racing usually feel that low range has a lot to offer. For instance in their *Jeep Four Wheel Drive Handbook,* James T. Crow and Cameron A. Warren emphasize that most 4 × 4 drivers "don't get enough use out of the lower set of gears in their transfer case. Low range is great! One of the best features of the 4WD vehicle! So use it. If there's a long, steep rise ahead, use low range. If you're following a sandy wash, use low range. If you're in doubt about the surface, use low range. . . .

"The greatest benefit of low range, to our way of thinking, is that it gives you better low-speed control than you can get even in first gear when in high range. You not only have better grade-climbing ability, but you can creep along, letting everything happen just as slowly and gently as possible. Grunching down a rocky defile you can ease up on one rock and down the other, letting yourself pick your way along. You may think that your regular first gear is plenty slow, but with it you have nothing like the control you have in low range.

"It even is good when you're trying to make better time when the road is bad. The moment you let up on the accelerator, the engine compression will slow you down, making it a lot easier on the brakes. Then, when you want to pick up speed again, there is plenty of torque available to move the rig right out. You also have three (or four) speeds in low range, of course, and the higher of these will propel you along at as much as 30-35 mph; yet you can slip back into second or first and be right back to a creep when you need to be."

One major difference in driving off the pavement as opposed to on the street is that there are so many different surfaces to consider. Your driving methods change depending on whether you're going over packed dirt, loose sand, mud, gravel, etc. There are also some variations in the way you drive over some surfaces, such as mud and sand, when those substances are *on* paved roadways. And, of course, there are still more changes in technique under various weather conditions, such as rain, snow or ice.

Mud is a good example. You could encounter it as a thin, slick film on top of a hard-packed dirt road after a rain or in thick, liquid bog form. In the case of the road film, it's advisable to keep a very light foot on the accelerator and a light grip on the wheel. The vehicle should be kept as high on the crown of the road as possible while avoiding sudden maneuvers that could cause it to move toward the shoulders where the mud might be deeper. As for a slide on muddy pavement in rainy or icy weather, if the vehicle starts doing that you should take your foot off the accelerator and steer in the direction of the slide until control is regained.

A driver coming to a patch of muddy ground, particularly off a regular track, would be wise to stop the vehicle, get out and look things over carefully. With a stick or rod, the driver should see how deep the mud is. If it's really deep or the bottom can't be found, the best move is either to find another way around it or drive back where you came from and find an alternate route.

While slightly different driving methods are needed for each type of mud, typically all require well controlled, steadily applied "go-ahead" power. Depending on which type of mud is to be traversed, you normally would select low range, using either first or second gear. If it's a boggy stretch, the maxim is that, once committed, don't hesitate, keep going. As experienced driver Jim Sprague puts it, "When you're slogging through the mud, the way to judge your progress is by the pace at which things move past you rather than what the needle on the speedometer says. Try to churn, churn and keep churning until you're back on firm footing. As long as you're moving, keep slogging. When you're not moving and the application of more throttle doesn't change the situation, get off the gas. Don't bury yourself any deeper than you have to."

Because it can sometimes take a lot of hard work and ingenuity to get out of the mud in the back country, it's generally a good idea to avoid untried patches of mud or other difficult terrain whenever possible. If you see tracks of another vehicle through a muddy area, it's best to stay in those rather than try to make new ones. Tell yourself, "If they got through, there has to be a bottom to it, so I should make it as well. That undisturbed patch that looks so much better may be *bottomless*."

With loose sand, as with mud, the technique is to use low range, maintain go-ahead, steady power and make no sudden changes in direction. As with mud, there are a number of types of sandy terrain and somewhat different approaches for each. For example, there's drift sand, wash sand and sand dunes. In the last category, there are ocean dunes and desert dunes to consider. Types of tires and tire pressures come into play. For operation on dunes only, many drivers prefer straight groove, high flotation tires. In general, any big tire can do the job. For dunes and for most sand travel, lowering tire pressure down to 8-10 pounds per square inch is favored.

As with mud, an operator coming upon a stretch of sand is advised to get out and inspect it to make sure it's passable and that the right technique is used. One trick Crow and Warren recommend for deciding on drivability is to walk into it with a heavy stride, sticking both heels down hard. "If your heels don't sink in, or sink in only enough to leave a definite heelprint, you can make it easily. If your heels sink in further, but you can still see a definite outline of your footprint, you can make it without trouble. If the sand simply slides right back in the marks you've made and leaves nothing but a vague oval in the sand, you may be in for trouble." In the latter case, if you probe it with a rod and can feel a reasonably hard area not too far down, the 4 × 4 probably still can get through. If you don't find a hard area, back away and look for another route.

Some general rules for driving in sand from Datsun are, "If it's a sandy wash you're going into, approach it at a steady clip; be sure you're in a low enough gear that you won't bog down, and drive steadily until you reach firm ground again. If you're running in sand dunes, try to make the slopes work for you. Study them, know where you want to go and how you're going to get there." As noted earlier, lowering the tire pressure is one precaution. Another is to avoid stopping in a hollow. The trick is to get enough momentum that any stop takes place on the top of a dune or on the downhill slope to make it easier to get going again. If you stop on the uphill slope, you may find yourself stuck.

Datsun cautions, "When coming to a stop in sand—and the same thing applies to snow or mud—keep the vehicle's wheels pointed straight ahead and let it roll to an easy stop, braking only lightly, if at all. This gives the tires a better chance of staying on top and minimizes the hump of sand to climb over before you can get underway again." As noted in the list of emergency equipment, sand mats are an important commodity. You put them under the wheels to give a firm surface to ride on in getting out of a sand obstacle.

For graded gravel surfaces, the rules are roughly the same as for hard-packed dirt roads, except that you don't usually have the problem of a mud slick on top in case of rain. The idea is to stay on the crown of the road as much as possible, since gravel at the edge may be looser and provide less stable footing. Jeep points out, "In loose gravel, as in deep snow or mud, you should maintain your momentum. Use your lowest transfer-case mode and keep a steady foot on the accelerator and a good grip on the wheel for directional stability."

On rocky stretches, the need is for low-range gear and very slow speed. In fact, the rule is to crawl up and creep down.

And sometimes even that is too fast. If you are driving with an automatic transmission, you'd use your brake to ease the vehicle down that rock it so deliberately climbed up. With a manual transmission, the approach is to let it "walk" into the rock against engine transmission. You'll kill the engine occasionally, but that's the way to do it.

An off-roader also must remember that when a large rock is ahead, it's important to overcome the normal impulse of pavement driving to straddle the obstacle and let it go underneath the vehicle. Instead, you must drive the wheel squarely over it. This way you know where the rock is and don't run the risk of its damaging the undercarriage or having the vehicle get stuck on it (referred to among 4×4 fans as "getting high centered").

On ice and snow there are more than a few varied conditions. These surfaces can be encountered in soft, hard, dry, wet, thin and deep formations, and it's possible to run into several of these conditions over a relatively short stretch of trail. The exact way to deal with each of these comes from experience that, in time, builds up the reflexes a driver needs to cope.

A Ford Motor Company engineer points out, "Snow is probably the most difficult and deceptive of all off-pavement surfaces, because it doesn't necessarily conform with the terrain it covers. Drive slowly and keep your momentum. If you feel yourself starting to bog down, try a gentle increase in accelerator pressure."

For deep snow and on ice, the consensus is that using low-range gears is in order. Where it's certain that the snow layer isn't too thick and is likely to remain fairly consistent, as on a well traveled road, high range gears can be used. Low range is the general choice on ice, particularly on a downhill slope, because it permits driving more cautiously and with less chance of breaking traction through too much gas pedal.

On deep snow, the primary concern is maintaining a steady, constant speed to keep the vehicle moving ahead without losing traction. Hard, packed snow is treated much like ice. Datsun advises, "Maintain a light touch, make all changes in speed and direction with great gentleness and, if the tires lose traction and start to slide, apply the brakes in gentle strokes, being careful not to lock up the wheels."

Crow and Warren observe, "There are some other driving pointers that apply almost exclusively to the snow country, such as rubbing a plug of tobacco or a raw onion on the windshield to keep it clear of snow and ice (but don't use your wipers too). Tire chains help on ice or slippery clay, but are much less useful on snow. Studded tires have proven their worth in winter and are highly thought of in Europe. The most important thing to remember is that you cannot steer a car with the brakes locked up, so learn to pump the brakes rapidly when you want to slow down or stop. Coming down an icy hill, get into low range and drive down very carefully. Avoid sudden applications of power or abrupt changes of direction whenever you come to a slippery stretch."

With water, as with many other potential obstacles, the old saw of looking before you leap again applies. As the Ford expert warns, "Driving into unknown water is like walking around blindfolded. That dropoff may only be an inch or two. Or it may be a precipice."

If the water proves to be deeper at any point than the vehicle hubs, the best strategy is to either backtrack or look for a better place to cross. Assuming the depth appears to be less than that, you still want to keep in low gear and move cautiously at a steady, straight-ahead pace. It's important not to stop broadside in running water. The high forces that water applies can easily sweep the vehicle downstream.

American Motors cautions, "Even when only a few inches of water are running, don't stop if you're on an unpaved surface. Moving water may wash the footing out from under your tires and make it impossible for you to get underway again. (The same principles apply if you're driving along the beach and get caught by a wave.) Don't stop. Keep moving. Head for the higher ground."

After getting free of water, it is important to dry out the brakes. This is done by driving with a light brake pressure and applying occasional additional pressure until the brake pedal responds normally. Something even an expert may overlook is the possible degrading effect the sand and silt present in muddy water can have on brake parts, wheel bearings and other items. After such exposure, a driver should inspect those systems carefully as soon as possible and, if necessary, make repairs.

Besides the different surfaces, four-wheel off-roading also can encompass a considerable amount of hill operation. Off-roaders talk of three "types" of hill terrain—uphill, downhill and sidehill. The meaning of uphill and downhill is pretty obvious. A sidehill operation simply refers to an instance where you drive across a slope, rather than straight up or down. Sidehill driving definitely isn't recommended. The only time to attempt it is when there's already an established road or trail or where there's no other way to get over or around the slope.

Typically on an uphill slope the rule is to drive straight up and not at an angle. It's not a bad idea to make a practice run to get the feel of the surface and figure out the right gear. Normally you would take a hill in low range using either first or second gear. In any case, you would want to back off a bit from the foot of the hill before going up to give yourself some room to work up some forward momentum. This is particularly desirable if the slope is made up of loose surface material.

On a practice run or on a full-blown attempt, if the wheels begin to spin, the first step is to apply a bit more gas to let them dig in slightly. Then clamp on the main brakes and also set the hand brake. After sitting for a moment to calm down, shift into reverse, carefully release the hand brake while letting out the clutch, then back down. The vehicle never should be in neutral, nor should the operator try to use the brakes for this maneuver. The idea is to keep the vehicle in gear and let the engine do the braking. The only time to use the brakes is if you feel the vehicle picking up too much speed.

Once on the bottom, try to assess the situation. If the gear was too high, choose a lower one. If there was a soft patch part way up, it's necessary to get up to a higher speed on the running start. Let's say you've figured your strategy out and are ready to "take" the hill. You put the car in gear, push down on the accelerator and move ahead, keeping a steady pace and maintaining good control. The idea is to have no hesitation, unless the wheels start to spin, in which case you can go through the backing maneuver as before. Assuming the 4×4 keeps going upward without problem, it's still important to approach the top of the hill in the right fashion. Just before getting to the top of the hill you ease off on the gas. This gives you the chance to see what's on the other side before you commit yourself to it. You wouldn't want to go full tilt into a hole or find a huge rock dead ahead.

On a steep downhill slope, the technique is much like that used in backing down a hill. The idea is to stay in a low gear and let the engine do the braking. Again the brakes only should be applied lightly to stem a breakneck downward rush.

Finally, we come back to sidehills. This can be one of the most hazardous types of driving anyone can attempt. It's okay for a stuntman, but definitely not a very good situation for almost anyone else. As a Jeep engineer puts it, "Surfaces on sidehills are deceptive. You may have been running along a ridge that seemed perfectly solid, but once you get into the sidehill it wanted to slip out from under you. The problem comes from the fact that when you're driving across a side slope the vehicle's weight is transferred to the lower side. Instead of having the weight distributed to the four tires, it's almost all on only two. This makes the vehicle want to slide down the hill sideways."

In fact, this force distribution could cause the vehicle to become unstable and begin to roll over. In most cases, the four-wheeler would slide before tipping over, but once it's sliding out of control, if the lower wheels hit an obstacle, the slide could turn into a possibly disastrous tumble.

A driver getting into that kind of fix has to keep his wits about him. The moment the car starts to slide, the nose must be immediately turned downhill. This helps transfer the weight to all four tires, moving the center of gravity back into the middle of the chassis.

As you can see, there's a lot more involved in driving a 4×4 or moving a motorcycle in off-road surroundings than meets the eye. But most of the difficulties can be avoided by common sense and a gradual build-up of experience before trying difficult excursions. And, the challenge and rewards of off-road activities make gaining the expertise well worth the effort.

5
OFF-ROAD RACING THRILLS

When it comes to off-road *racing,* some of the guidelines mentioned in the last chapter no longer apply. It isn't true that off-road daredevils throw caution to the winds—many of the basic considerations we've just discussed still are observed. But certainly when it's a matter of trying to get from point A to point B ahead of a competitor, a racer will take more chances and generally go at higher speeds than a recreational driver or rider. Where speeds of twenty or thirty miles per hour might be considered high for the average person's off-road activities, professional racers may hit speeds of 100 miles per hour or better over heart-pounding stretches of boulder-strewn paths or sharply changing hill country. Even over treacherous courses like those used in Baja events of SCORE'S Parker 400 with its bone-chilling Thunder Alley, the average start-to-finish speeds of expert bikers and four-wheelers may exceed 50 mph.

However, it also should be pointed out that the bikes and vehicles used for such grueling tests are much more ruggedly outfitted than the stock off-road motorcycle or automobile. For instance, where a standard four-wheel truck might have four to eight shock absorbers, a vehicle used in a major off-road event might have more than a dozen. (And the emergency kit for such racing would include a number of spare shocks as well.)

And participants in long-course events like the Parker 400, Baja 1000 and Baja International don't just arrive the night before and move onto the starting grid. Experienced racers and their teams do what is called "pre-running"—driving the course ahead of time to take careful note of the features and obstacles. If you were to go to the hotel rooms of experts like Mickey Thompson, Roger Mears, Walker Evans or Ivan Stewart the night before a big race, you would see walls, tables and even floors covered with maps and charts showing in elaborate detail the race route with dangerous pitfalls marked. From this the team works out its strategy—where to push down on the accelerator, where to ease back on the throttle and, equally important, what spots to go around or avoid.

One problem with long-course off-road racing, naturally, is that spectator participation is quite limited. Onlookers can watch the starting phase, which may include a parade of the different bikes and vehicles like the one that takes place down the main street of Reno, Nevada, before the Mint 400 gets underway, and can be there to see the finishers straggle in at the finish line, and can possibly find some vantage points along the course to see entries go by without having too good an idea of who's leading. But there's no chance to see the entire race except, perhaps, from a low-flying airplane. Even with all those drawbacks, the number of people following such off-road events grew during the 1960s and early 1970s, but this still amounted to a small fraction of the auto-racing public.

All this changed with the advent in the 1970s of short-course off-road racing. The man who pioneered this was Mickey Thompson, whose exploits in drag racing and world-speed-record attempts brought him international recognition in the 1960s. During the 1972 Mint 400, a race which, for a change, he hadn't entered, he went up in his private plane and got a panoramic view of the action. Below him, motorcycles, dune buggies, pickup trucks and other classes of off-road machines charged across the desert, sending plumes of dust into the air while engaging in various races within the overall race. It was, he decided, challenging, exciting, breathtaking—potentially one of the best spectator events in the nation if it could somehow be compressed into a conventional-size racing layout.

Almost immediately he set about making his dream of large-audience off-road racing a reality. But first he did the necessary "pre-running." He considered the kinds of vehicles involved, consulted with veteran race planners and spent a lot of time just thinking about what would be needed in terms of facilities and organization for his project. One of the first things required, he decided, was a simple numbering system for classes of vehicles to replace the varying and often confusing designations used by racing groups in the United States and elsewhere. The category system he devised within a few years became the accepted one for off-road racing throughout North America. As of the mid-1980s, the organization he founded in 1973 to develop spectator-oriented off-road racing (Short Course Off-Road Enterprises, which later became known as SCORE International) sponsored races for some twenty-four categories.

These comprise (with class numbers in parentheses): (1) unlimited single-seat vehicles (usually dune buggies); (1-1600) single-seat VW dune buggies with 1600-cc engines; (2-1600) two-seat VW dune buggies with 1600-cc engines; (2) unlimited two-seat vehicles (usually dune buggies); (3S) production four-wheel-drive vehicles, short wheelbase; (3L) production four-wheel-drive vehicles, long wheelbase; (4) modified four-wheel-drive vehicles; (5) Baja Bugs (modified VW sedans); (5-1600) Baja Bugs restricted to 1600-cc VW engines; (6) production two-wheel-drive automobiles; (7) mini-pickups; (8) full-size pickups and other utility vehicles; (9) single-seat 1200-cc VW-powered dune buggies; (10) two-seat 1200-cc VW-powered dune buggies; (11) showroom stock VW sedans; (18) single-seat 1835-cc VW-powered dune buggies; (20) motorcycles, 125-cc and under; (21) motorcyles, 126–250 cc; (22) motorcycles, unlimited; (23) three-wheelers, 125 cc and under; (30) motorcycles, ridden by competitors thirty and under; (33) three-wheelers, 250 cc and under; (38) motorcycles, ridden by competitors over thirty; (43) three-wheelers unlimited.

The core of Thompson's idea, once he'd sorted out the racing combinations, was to simulate a full-size off-road race in a relatively small area. This was essentially the same approach used in the motorcycle motocross events that draw huge crowds to specially prepared layouts in sports arenas and stadiums. The off-road course can be designed for such places, though typically it is now installed in larger venues, such as automotive raceways or horse-racing ovals at fairgrounds which permit greater diversity of terrain features.

The first location chosen for a SCORE race was Riverside International Raceway, Riverside, California, a track well known to race fans as the site of major sports-car, stock-car and Indy-type events. Unluckily, the Thompson promotion was scheduled for October 5–7, 1973, which turned out to be right in the middle of the energy crisis caused by the Arab oil embargo. On that very weekend, Southern California service station operators closed down as part of a two-day boycott protesting the price-supply squeeze they were being subjected to by oil companies. Fearful of running out of gas, many fans stayed away from the debut SCORE race (called the AC-Delco RV Spectacular) and caused Mickey to cancel plans for similar events in other locales.

However, Mickey and SCORE persevered and, as the oil crunch eased in the mid-1970s, the Riverside series was established as one of the bellwethers of the growing off-road movement. By the 1980s, it was drawing upwards of 50,000 people a year to witness superstars from all major SCORE classes competing for prizes totaling hundreds of thousands of dollars. Thompson by then had long stepped down as head of the SCORE operation. In fact, he was busy organizing other short-course events of his own. The destinies of SCORE were directed by Sal Fish, a one-time editor of *Hot Rod* magazine, whom Thompson had picked to head SCORE in the mid-1970s.

The Riverside event in the 1980s was known as the Bridgestone SCORE Off-Road World Championship. It comprised a series of races, including the Challenge of Champions, an eleven-lap race for unlimited single-seaters open to sixty drivers for what SCORE claimed to be the "largest one-class purse in off-road racing"; the Pernod Heavy Metal Challenge, eleven laps for 4,000-pound pickup trucks open to thirty drivers; the eleven-lap Datsun Mini-Metal Challenge; plus many short races for a variety of four-wheel vehicles, three-wheelers, and eight classes of two-wheel motorcycles.

The course used for these hard-charging, often wheel-to-wheel races is a 1.5 mile-per-lap, 1.5 mile layout simulating Baja type terrain. Drivers have to work their way through ten turns, many jumps, and a long, reverse-camber hillside known as Thompson Ridge which became notorious for rolling cars over. Surface conditions change constantly from smooth pavement to washboard, hard-packed dirt, mud holes and bumps.

As it happened, the Riverside event remained the only short-course one directly sponsored by SCORE. Of the six events on the SCORE Grand Prix schedule in the 1980s, five were long-course ones. In fact, while there were good cash prizes at Riverside, drivers and bike riders taking part weren't given points toward the Off-Road Grand Prix Championship trophies awarded annually by SCORE in association with the French beverage firm of Pernod. Points for those honors only could be achieved in the longer races. (While SCORE is a direct sponsor of the Grand Prix series, it expanded its role in off-road activities over the years to become the sanctioning body for races all over the world. These included events across the United States, plus some in Canada, Africa, and an annual event held on the island of Guam in the South Pacific.)

The first SCORE move into long-course operations came in the mid-1970s. In the 1980s, the Grand Prix series included three races on the Baja. These are the Pernod San Felipe 250, typically held in March; the Pernod Baja International, run from Ensenada on the Pacific Ocean to a point on the Gulf of California and back; and the classic Pernod Baja 1000, a 985-mile, exhausting marathon down the finger-like Baja peninsula from Ensenada to La Paz in November. (The distance from Tijuana south to La Paz is a little over 1000 miles, hence the Baja 1000 designation. When the official starting point moved down to Ensenada, the total race distance shrank a bit, but the time-honored name was retained.)

The first organized Baja race, the Mexican 1000, got underway on October 31, 1967, with sixty-eight entrants in the starting grid in Tijuana. First to cross the finish line in La Paz in a time of twenty-seven hours, thirty-eight minutes was the team of Vic Wilson and Ted Mangels in a Meyers

Manx. The publicity given that race inspired the Mint Hotel in Nevada to initiate its Mint 400 in 1968. Organized long-course off-road racing was on its way.

Taking part in both those events in the late 1960s and early 1970s was Mickey Thompson, who found the driving among the most exciting he'd experienced in years of racing. He also began to see the potential as well as the early shortcomings of the sport, an understanding that led to the establishment of SCORE. But for all that, his fondest dream was to win the Baja 1000. In some ways his Baja 1000 saga symbolized the frustrations and challenges of off-road racing. Though Mickey had honors enough for a dozen stars in his long racing career and pioneered many breakthroughs in equipment and automotive technology, he seemed to be jinxed off-road, particularly by the winding, punishing Mexican course. Year after year he entered with advanced-design, top-quality 4 × 4 vehicles, took great pains in the pre-running, and left the starting line as one of the favorites. Year after year he surged to the front in the first part of the race only to have his equipment crippled by part failures or unexpected road hazards.

Coming into 1982, in his mid-fifties, he was in the twilight of his career as an active driver. Starting in the late 1970s, he assembled funds for filming a documentary of his life in auto sports, dreaming of climaxing the movie with a 4 × 4 first in the Baja 1000 as the highlight of thirty years in racing. Each year he arranged to have a large crew of movie cameramen focus on his part in the race in hopes of getting the desired film-ending footage and each time something went wrong. Though still taking part in the Baja in 1982, he found the money for the movie project dwindling. He decided it was best to use what was left to complete the film rather than finance another seemingly hopeless filming of his Baja run. While he made his usual extensive preparations for racing, he had no provisions for a special film crew to follow his vehicle.

The irony wasn't lost on his friends or the press when his part in the 1982 Baja became history. A little after 3 A.M. on November 5, 1982, the first 4 × 4 flashed past the finish line in La Paz. It was the Raceco VW piloted by Mickey and his co-driver Terry Smith. The vehicle had held first place wire-to-wire with an elapsed time of 19 hours, 40 minutes, 23.84 seconds, an average speed over the course of 49.993 mph. From his filmmaking standpoint it was very disappointing, but in all other ways it was a satisfying triumph, putting to rest the idea that Thompson, a perennial early leader, was incapable of finishing a long-course off-road race.

Actually, there were plenty of moments when Thompson felt fate might be catching up with him again. Some of those related to difficulties posed by the course, but another was a matter of logistics—hooking up with co-driver Smith. The reason this was necessary was that the owner of the VW, Jack Motley, who originally was scheduled to be the driver of record with Mickey as co-driver, was called away on business at the last minute. He decided to leave the car in the race, designating Mickey as driver of record with someone else to become co-driver. Thus Mickey came close to not even being in the race.

As Mickey's wife Trudy related in the press room after the race, "Jack Motley called us in Ensenada and told us who our co-driver would be. He told us we would change at Rosarito, which is after El Cruzero. On our pre-run we looked for Terry Smith there but didn't find him. So when Mickey started the race, he didn't know for sure if Terry would be there to relieve him. We agreed he would look for Terry there and if he didn't find him he would just keep going until he did. Jack Motley told Terry to meet us at Rosarito, twenty miles down the course. I was driving Mickey's pickup looking for Terry. I met him coming the other way going into Rosarito and we both stopped and got together. I followed him to where they made the switch."

When Thompson came into that town, Trudy flagged him down. Her motions made him finally understand she'd found Smith, but it was almost another disastrous episode. "I almost ran into her," Thompson told the press briefing.

Reminiscing a bit after the victory, Smith said, "It's the greatest feeling coming into La Paz and seeing those lights, especially after those mud pools below San Ignacio, a beach stretch which was flooded by high tide. Mickey siliconed the engine to keep it dry, and if it weren't for his tires (specially designed) I would never have made it to victory lane. I might still be out there."

Thompson added, "You know how high tide leaves water holes. I got stuck too, near Gonzaga Bay. I had run through the rock pile [a rugged stretch called Three Sisters] and I got in the mud and couldn't get out. I was down twenty-five minutes and couldn't get out. I was out of the car twenty-five times before El Arco and siliconed the engine."

The special tires Mickey designed for the car contributed a lot to the car's performance. A good part of his reputation in the racing field was based on the innovations he came up with to improve vehicle capabilities under difficult conditions. In the past, he often took wry pleasure from the way some of those innovations contributed to the success of other racers in events he himself had to drop out of.

With the new tire design, the VW made the journey all the way down the Baja without a single tire change. The tires gave exceptionally good mud performance, Smith suggested, because of the tread and wall design. "The tread curves around the tire and up the side. It gives just enough traction to keep you going even in mud."

Still, the demanding pace needed to win the class left its scars on the car. Thompson joked about its condition when it reached La Paz. "I gave [Terry] a perfectly good race car and he gave me a junk pre-runner. The valves are burnt. It took me fourteen hours to get from La Paz back to Ensenada [on paved road]. Every ten miles I had to stop and get water."

During his odyssey, Thompson recalled a stretch where he had to cope with splattering mud and water near Gonzaga Bay. "About the time I got the mud out of my eyes, some guys landed in an airplane to help me put out the fire. That was funny. I set the fire to burn off the water. The second time I did it, it blazed pretty high and I had to start driving the car to get enough wind to put it out. But they thought I was burning up."

Among the many entrants in the motorcycle sections of the race was sports writer Timothy Carlson of the Los Angeles *Herald Examiner* who became enamored of the idea of completing the whole run after covering the 1979 event. At the press briefing he recalled, "I came down here with [cyclist]Tracy Valenta on a pre-run and did a story and the race became an obsession. I put a picture that was used with the story up on my wall. It shows [motorcycle racer] Bobby Ferro driving through those Cardon cactus . . . I watched the fluidity of Larry Roeseler, how he makes ever so slight a move and he comes so close to disaster; so slight a move, that's all, very subtle, but it becomes important and makes him that much faster than an ordinary man riding a motorcycle."

In 1981, Carlson bought his own motorcycle with the idea of starting to prepare for the Baja, but "I broke both wrists the first time I was out on the bike. I was out of action for two and a half months in excruciating pain. I had a compound fracture of the left wrist, but I did a lot of exercise and eventually I got stronger as I got well.

"I grew up in Daytona Beach, Florida, watching Curtis Turner slide through the turns on the old beach course. I was interested in what made him and those other stock car racers do what they did so well. They showed me such initiative. They had faith in their abilities. And they were so totally involved in what they did. In my job I became interested in other forms of racing and saw the same qualities in other drivers, but I knew I could never race at Indianapolis or in Formula I. But off-road racing—that was the great leveler of humanity. I wouldn't be out of place in Baja. I invested ten thousand dollars out of my take-home pay for the gear, the trailer, the expense of the pre-run. One reason I wanted to be here besides the thrill of racing was the heartbreaking beauty of the Baja.

"I'm the measure of the average man in this race. I have average reactions and average endurance. I did a story on Bobby Ferro. In fact, it was his last race here. I did a section at half the speed he did. I raced at sixty percent of the speed of expert riders like Johnson and Baker. It was terrifyingly fast for me! It was a question of making the right moves. My partner Kent Richardson flipped in practice and was knocked unconscious right in front of our 'sponsor' Malcolm Smith. It shook him up." (Smith, who has a company that makes racing uniforms, provided suits for Carlson and his teammate.)

Carlson didn't win in 1982. He finished fourteenth in his class, which meant that quite a few cyclists of different race categories came in ahead of him. But for the many "weekend" racers, as is the case for most people who run in marathons, the goal wasn't to win, but to take part and, the most exultant achievement of all, to cross the finish line.

Along with racing superstars like Mears, Evans and Stewart, people like Carlson take part in long-course races and in amateur or semi-amateur segments of short-course meets. Even for the many who don't complete the race, there's the thrill of daring the unknown and the adventures and misadventures worth talking about for years afterward. In fact, in all the off-road events, only a fraction of the starters make it all the way. In a typical early 1980s Mint 400, for example, 500 would start and only about 100 would complete the rock-strewn, sandy, kidney-shaped course. Commenting on a typical Mint 400, race director K. J. Howe said after a race, "It looked like the desert in North Africa after a meeting between Patton and Rommel."

The same holds true for the Parker 400, another of the Grand Prix events run by SCORE International, which covers some 400 miles from a starting point in the California desert to Parker, Arizona. It takes not only skill, stamina and rugged equipment, but dogged determination to get your machine safely over a route which, as Los Angeles *Times* staff writer Gene Chandler recalled from his experiences as a participant, includes the following:

"An incredibly bumpy and rutted dirt road . . . renowned for its 'whoop-de-do's'—a series of bumps raised by thousands of trips in the previous weeks by vehicles 'pre-running,' or attempting to learn the course.

"Foglike dust clouds kicked up by rivals that blotted out the course with (usually) little wind to blow it away.

"Problems of passing. The only way is to catch up with the racer ahead and 'eat' his dust. A driver must try to bump over the tricky terrain faster than a competitor he can barely see. And when he has caught up, he often has to 'nerf'—or ram—the car ahead to 'persuade' him to pull over to allow a pass."

Under SCORE's organizational plans for a race like the Parker 400, the vehicles move out on the course by categories. The initial honors go to the dirt bikes with unlimiteds roaring out to get things underway followed at thirty-second intervals by other motorcycle groups. After an hour and a half wait, the green light is given the first four-wheel class, unlimited single-seaters, followed by unlimited two-seaters, four-wheel drives, limited engine buggy classes, Baja bugs, large and small pickups, production sedans, and somewhat modified "stock" VWs.

Driving in one of the buggy classes, Chandler sought to put as much distance as possible between himself and the "heavy metal" pickup group before getting to Thunder Alley, forty-five miles from the starting line. As he noted, "Though Thunder Alley comprises only fourteen miles of the old power-line road, I knew from being passed there in previous races that the speed differential between my eighty-five-mile-per-hour buggy and the trucks could mean trouble. For although the road is straight, it's rutty and dusty and has enough bumps to keep the knuckles white, especially when a big pickup looms out of the dust in your rear-view mirror and starts closing on your bumper with the old power line poles whipping by only a few feet on your left." If one of those hulking monsters should swerve a bit, he knew, the smaller car could be crushed like an insect against a pole.

It's just another hazard of off-road racing. In this case, running "scared" proved costly, because Chandler misjudged a bump, flew high in the air and ended up with the car on its side where, fortunately unhurt, he had to wait many precious minutes before he could flag someone down to help right the buggy. He jumped in, got into gear and started off, only to find that one of the shocks was broken.

"I jumped out again, opened the hood, took out my tools and unhooked the extra shock I carry like almost everyone else.... Replacing the shock, which was boiling hot from the race, cost another precious ten minutes. Then I groaned when the leading big pickup, driven by off-road star Ivan Stewart, came thundering by. I was only about five miles from Thunder Alley and now was barely in front of the other twenty-one of those 500-horsepower beasts."

In Thunder Alley, every few minutes another heavy metal truck zoomed by. "I always pulled over to my right to let them by so *they* had to pass next to those menacing solid power poles.... Once by, the trucks would spin their tires in the road as they floored it, showering my supposedly unbreakable helmet visor with sand, gravel, and even rocks—my car has no windshield. This forced me to back off, as I was left in a twenty-foot visibility cloud of dust."

In this case, Chandler kept going on, but at a more sedate pace, which probably was just as well. "The road ran through ten-mile-per-hour volcanic rock fields that can cut tires, interspersed with foot-deep silt beds that can suffocate engine and driver alike. Then came high-speed stretches with 'sweeper' turns with berms—banked ruts for wheels—that off-road cars can take at well over freeway speeds because it's like running on rails...."

In the final twenty miles of his part of the race, Chandler recalled, "I was stuck in the dust behind some of the big rock-showering pickups as the course wound into Chemehuevi Wash, a narrow, gravel-bottomed canyon through some hills. Only fifteen feet wide at times, it had ruts more than a foot deep and blind corners—not the kind of place to attempt to get someone three times your size to pull over."

After reaching the Colorado River on the California-Arizona border, most drivers turn the car over to a co-driver, in Chandler's case his brother, Michael. A professional race driver, Michael brought the car home to Parker finishing a respectable ninth. Again, the two drivers felt, as Carlson had in the Baja, that bringing the vehicle the entire route from start to finish over such a demanding course was a major, satisfying accomplishment.

Compressing that kind of obstacle course into a short-form operation was hardly an easy task for Mickey Thompson, Sal Fish and SCORE International. In a way, eliminating many of the long straight stretches of long-course layouts while crowding a series of difficult turns and obstacles into a small space promised to pose new problems for racers. But professional drivers welcomed the challenge to their reflexes and ingenuity, particularly since having large paying audiences promised to provide sizable prize money.

In 1979, Mickey Thompson demonstrated that meaningful off-road 4 × 4 racing could be held in regular sports stadiums as well as in automotive raceways when he produced the first Off-Road Championship Grand Prix in the Los Angeles Coliseum. The Coliseum, home for many years to the Los Angeles Rams and later the Los Angeles Raiders, the University of Southern California and UCLA football teams and, for a while, the Los Angeles Dodgers, had been used for motocross races in the past. But it seemed asking too much to expect that a good off-road course for 4 × 4s as well as for cycles could be crammed onto the playing field. Mickey was undaunted. He trucked in tons of dirt and used a phalanx of earth-moving machines to shape the soil into a three-quarter-mile track. The course took competitors up a thirty-eight-degree incline section built over the seats at the peristyle end of the field, through the marble peristyle and back down over a sixty-foot dropoff to the stadium floor.

It was called the most incredible race track of its kind ever built. During the two years the event was held, in 1979 and 1980, huge crowds filled the arena to watch the top names in all off-road classes, from motorcycles to heavy metal pickups, perform awesome, sometimes death-defying maneuvers for some of the largest amounts of prize money ever offered off-roaders. Obviously it wasn't a place for novices, but it suggested some of the fantasies average drivers could aspire to while running in long-course events.

Since the program included many motorcycle races, you might ask what the difference was between those and motocross competition. The answer is that the course was set up to simulate desert-type racing which is quite different from other motorcycle events. For one thing, the race calls for a wider range of techniques on the part of the rider which, in turn, demands different bike design features than for other type races.

As Rik Paul emphasized in a program note for Thompson's Coliseum Grand Prix, "Though there are several other forms of cross-country bike racing, none combine all the elements found in a desert event. Since it is an all-out speed race across unknown, desolate and often difficult terrain covering hundreds of miles, a racer must be adept at all phases of dirt biking. It requires the wide-open speed, delicate finesse and balance of motocross, as well as the ability to maintain intense, lengthy concentration to read and negotiate unfamiliar terrain, the reflexes to react to sudden obstacles, and the mental stamina to stay alert and competitive over long hours of brutal physical exertion. You also need the mechanical savvy to keep the machine running when the consequences include being stranded miles from civilization."

He stressed that this type of off-road racing exerts many more shocks and forces on a bike than typical motocross running. This is one reason desert race bikes use very long travel suspensions—in the 1980 models travel suspension on both front and rear is about eleven inches.

"In addition, since the racer often spends the better part of a day atop his bike, the comfort factor, too, becomes critical. Finally, and most important of all, while being competitively fast, the bike also must be absolutely reliable. Every mechanical detail must be gone over and double-checked, and numerous precautions must be taken to guard against the thick dust, sudden rocks, flying pebbles and other hazards.

"Modifications usually are made to stock bikes to adapt them for the desert. This often includes larger gas tanks for the long races, quartz halogen lights for nighttime races like the Baja 1000 and many smaller changes intended to make the bike stronger and more durable, such as stronger tires, shocks, rims and spokes. Radical engine modifications are mostly bypassed to maintain maximum reliability."

Of course, Paul is talking about full-scale desert races rather than short-course runs. However, typical off-road courses are much more demanding than conventional motocross layouts and many of the factors he spotlights come into play.

An examination of the different cycle race classifications from short-course meetings to full long-course events indicates the favored designs cover a displacement range from around 125 cc to 650 cc. Except where otherwise specified, most riders opt for two-wheelers with displacements of 250 to 650 cc to gain a good combination of power and ruggedness. Compared to the specifications of street bikes, those displacements might seem rather low, but the bikes offer combinations of power-to-weight ratios that give the best performance to meet off-road conditions.

While the Los Angeles Coliseum events went well in 1979–80, Mickey Thompson felt he could achieve even more crowd-pleasing results if he could find places to install permanent short-course off-road tracks rather than ones that had to be taken down right after an event was completed. From his Coliseum experience as well as his participation and observation of all kinds of races over the years, he wanted to design a permanent track that could provide more exciting possibilities than ever before for drivers as well as spectators. During 1981 he took time out to consider possible sites and to think about what seemed desirable in an advanced off-road short-course layout.

Looking around his home area, he concluded a perfect spot for his new track would be the infield of the horseracing oval at the Los Angeles County Fairgrounds at Pomona. Most of the year the facility was empty, being used only for a few weeks in the early fall while the fair was in progress and for occasional special events other times in the year. He suggested to county officials that having an off-road course wouldn't interfere with any other events and would provide an extra source of much needed revenue for the county. He got the go-ahead on a provisional basis—he could install the course and run two meetings in 1982 to see if it worked well. If it did, he could get a contract for more events on an annual basis.

The contract was signed in January 1982 and Thompson and the design firm of Dick Dahn & Associates went to work. Week after week the track configuration took shape, a winding, hilly course with all kinds of turns and carefully placed bumps four feet or more high. The layout featured some innovations that had been taking shape in Thompson's mind for a long time, the most novel of which was the "any groove" concept.

Typically in dirt-track racing, where the track simply is

laid down and opened to action, in a short time drivers and riders find there is one part of the surface that provides the best traction and fastest pace. This is called the "groove." As vehicles jockey for position, there's only one fast lane available. Mickey's idea was to engineer the course so there would be no way for a single groove to develop. By doing this and making the track wide enough (the Pomona course has a minimum width of 36 ft), he reasoned, it would be possible to have the excitement of three abreast racing. Such a setup also more closely approximates desert racing where the wide open space in portions of the course can accommodate many vehicles running parallel to each other.

One thing Thompson did was to make the inside lane a little higher than the rest of the course. Normally the inside lane on a conventional track is the fastest and the place where the "groove" typically is found. By elevating this track section, though, he made it just a bit slower than it normally would be compared to the other lanes to help even things out for all the lanes. He stressed, "We didn't want a 'follow-the-leader' track. We wanted to force drivers to use the whole track and really race."

Besides equalizing the lane speeds of all drivers, he pointed out, "This new three-lane concept allows for more controlled passing and should cut down on vehicle contact considerably. Combining that with carefully placed built-in bumps gives a layout that offers the feel and excitement of long-course racing where thousands of people can watch the race from start to finish."

Some of the steps he took for short-course competition outraged off-road purists, but Thompson was sure it would be beneficial to everybody in the field in the long run. For instance, for the Pomona permanent track, he had the dirt treated with chemicals to cut down on dust clouds and flying particles and had the vehicles fitted with mufflers.

"Everybody said don't do it," Thompson said. "They said you'll ruin it. But who needs dust? And the noise? You can hear the engine now. You can hear the rpms without the loud bang-bang noise. Our surveys had shown that the people didn't like not being able to hear the public address system. Now you can hear what's going on."

It all seemed to work out as Thompson had predicted. The two inaugural events in 1982 drew large, enthusiastic crowds that watched spine-tingling dogfights between top professionals (including Mickey's son, Danny, an expert driver of 4×4s who is also adept at motorcycle racing). Also indicating that dynasties aren't uncommon in off-road racing was the presence in several races of Jeff MacPherson, whose father Joe's exploits in 1981 had won him SCORE International's "Man of the Year" award.

Taking part as well was rock star Ted Nugent, a heavy metal music exponent, who had gotten into off-road racing after Mickey Thompson invited him to take part in the Celebrity Challenge phase of the 1979 Los Angeles Coliseum Off-Road Championship. After that, Nugent became so engrossed in the sport that he entered every off-road long-course race he could fit in with his performing schedule, including many SCORE events, the Mint 400 and the Coors/USA Off-Road Championships in Colorado Springs, Colorado.

Public interest in the SCORE/Bridgestone and Pomona short-course events helped spark promoters throughout the United States to sponsor similar competitions. In the 1980s, more and more races were held on specially prepared courses from the East Coast to the Mid- and Southwest. It could be said that off-road racing had truly become a mature spectator sport.

The significance was pointed out by Thompson in the program for one of his Pomona meetings. "There was a time when viewing an off-road race was more of a crusade than a simple one-day outing. If you wanted to witness a major off-road race, it could mean driving 300 to 1000 miles in your motorhome, camper or van, making food and clothing provisions for three days to a week or more, and having plenty of cash on hand to allow for emergencies. With short-course off-road racing that all has changed."

Which didn't mean that traditional long-course off-road race popularity had slipped. Indeed, Thompson emphasized, "That option is still available to the off-road fan as evidenced by the fact that desert [long-course] off-road racing continues to grow and prosper. The adventure of visiting new places, the excitement of the racing, the camaraderie of other fans, racers and pit crews are rewarding experiences for those who don't mind the extra planning and occasional inconvenience."

Some of those experiences are available on a less structured level via the expanding activities of off-road clubs and organizations, as we'll see.

6
GRASS ROOTS OFF-ROADING

As we've emphasized, while one of the attractions of off-roading is the chance to get away from the hurried pace of urban life, it's also a potentially dangerous thing to go into the back country alone. But, conveniently, as people get into off-roading, they often don't like to have just one "buddy," but a number of them. Of course, off-roading has long been a good way to have family get-togethers and, increasingly, groups of people who enjoy off-road activities have banded together to form off-road clubs. Today there are all manner of off-road organizations in existence and, in addition, companies involved in making or servicing particular types of off-road equipment are organizing special off-road outings.

A list of clubs is presented in the Appendix. Since local clubs tend to change addresses and phone numbers from time to time, and since there always are a few dropping out while new ones are formed, specific addresses of these aren't given. However, you can find out the name of one in your vicinity by contacting the state- or area-wide associations whose addresses and phone numbers are shown. If there is no club in your area and you'd like to help start one, contact one of the national organizations for information on how best to do it. Among the largest of these are: the American Motorcyclist Association, Box 141, Westerville, OH 43081, telephone (614) 891-2425; American All-Terrain Vehicle Association (for three-wheel vehicles), Box 1522, Westerville, OH 43081, telephone (614) 891-2425; and the United Four-Wheel Drive Associations, 2119 S. Birch St., Denver, CO 80222, telephone (303) 753-1464. You can find other central organizations in the Appendix. Some of the nationwide organizations provide detailed guides to club formation; for example, the American Motorcyclist Association has a publication titled *How and Why to Form a Motorcycle Club*.

One of the things clubs offer is the forum for off-road fans to get together and exchange stories of back-country adventures, sometimes falling into the "tall tale" classification, and to show off home-made modifications of their off-road vehicles. As you'll find out if you, your family or friends get involved, most off-roaders are born tinkerers and get much enjoyment out of modifying or changing whatever vehicle is in the garage or driveway at a given time.

In fact, many people have gotten into four-wheel driving by converting old two-wheel-drive cars into four-wheel-drive systems. One way to make such a transition is to take a vehicle like a Volkswagen "Bug," a Volvo, or similar car, and cut and reweld the chassis to make room for a live axle. An alternative is to take off the original body and attach it to a pre-assembled 4×4 system. There are kits available to do this and there are companies in business to produce such conversions on an assembly-line basis.

Some four-wheel-drive fans like to take classic cars and convert them from two- to four-wheel drive. Among such conversions that have been displayed in classic-car rallies in recent years were reworked 1941 and 1945 Chevy pickups, 1949 Willys Jeepsters, 1950 Studebaker Commander Sedans, 1955 Chrysler New Yorkers, and what is considered by many to have been the first four-wheel-drive van, a 1957 vehicle built by Milwaukee automotive designer Brooks Stevens from an FC-150 Jeep truck. There are plenty of vintage car and motorcycle clubs in existence (one example is the Vintage Chevrolet Club of America) for classic model 4 × 4 enthusiasts to join.

A person who knows something about the way vehicles are assembled can get into four-wheel-drive systems by putting together a 4×4 car or truck from old parts. Parts can be obtained from junkyards or from companies dealing in such equipment. The project should be based on a vehicle that's been on the market long enough for disabled or worn-out versions to be available for very low cost or found in local junkyards. There are publications dealing with such activities, such as the *Vintage Auto Almanac*, which lists parts companies and old car clubs, and newspapers and magazines like *Old-Car Weekly*, *Cars & Parts* and *Car Exchange*. Besides these, various price guides to used parts are published; these might be tracked down in the automotive section of the local book store.

If you decide to do something like this, the watchword, as is true for off-roading in general, is clear thinking and careful advance planning. One thing that's required is a lot of reading and research. Even if you're not ready to build or rebuild your own off-road vehicle, it can be fun to collect information and draw up plans for such a dream system. You could, for instance, work out the design and assemble a small-scale model, something manufacturers do at the start of a new program. They have design research groups that make scale models of proposed systems (whether two-, three- or four-wheelers) and make scale models for study purposes before committing large sums of money for production.

A good first step in your program is to collect as much information as possible on vehicle types that interest you. You can get literature on new models by writing manufacturers or getting brochures from new car or cycle showrooms. For older designs, see if your local public library has books giving design and performance data about old vehicles. Also, a good form of literary research is to leaf through automotive and motorcycle magazines, many of which have special issues dealing with various classes of two-, three- and four-wheel vehicles. A large publishing house like Petersen Publishing of Los Angeles comes out with annual encyclopedic issues, covering not only classes of vehicles and cycles, but important subsystems like engines and components.

The initial goal of such research is to decide on what vehicle or vehicles to base your project. Besides reading about what's been produced here and abroad over the years, you might get tips from friends involved in off-road activities or from mechanics at local garages or manufacturers' service stations. If you live in a large urban area where annual shows like the SCORE International Off-Road

Equipment show or annual new automotive and/or motorcycle shows take place, those are great places to get a look at what's going on in the off-road field.

It's interesting that SCORE also sponsors a competition for model builders at the annual equipment show. Called the RC Racing News/SCORE Radio Controlled Off-Road World Championship, it features a miniature Baja-type dirt course complete with jumps, bumps and a water hole for racing scale model vehicles. In this successor to the old-time slot-car racing competition, several hundred battery-powered scale models of real off-road racers take part. Most of these are constructed with meticulous care by hobbyists. The models feature operating versions of things like independent suspensions and special shock absorbers. Some of the 1980s designs had tiny, perfectly working advanced gas pressure shocks, like those pioneered by Bilstein Corporation of America.

If model building is your interest, you can find information about scale designs in some of the hobby books devoted to such topics. Of course, many models of off-road vehicles (including motorcycles) are available in kit form in hobby stores. But it's more fun if you can work out the design and build it yourself, and it's great preparation for going on later to building or modifying full-scale equipment. A hobby store is a good place to find the titles of magazines covering off-road modeling.

As far as full-scale systems are concerned, cost naturally is a major factor for someone who's going to do the building job by himself or herself (or as a team). There are publications available, like the *Old Cars Price Guide*, that give some idea of the going price for older vehicles. You can find used vehicles for sale listed in the classified sections of newspapers and in special publications dealing with all kinds of used items. (These publications are often offered free—the people inserting ads pay for the issue.) In Southern California, there is a paper called *The Recycler* that lists used products for sale, and there are similar publications in other major cities. Then, as we indicated before, there's that old reliable of home mechanics, the junkyard, which is a happy hunting ground for everything from complete vehicles in various stages of disrepair to all manner of spare parts. A tour through the local junkyard can shed light on probable costs involved.

Once you've narrowed your interest to a few likely makes, the availability of usable parts is an important consideration. Again it's a case of getting as much data as possible. The junkyard is as good a starting point as any. In fact, rather than just go to any automobile junkyard, you might see if there's one around that specializes in reclaiming parts from off-road vehicles. A telephone book yellow pages is a good place to look for one, or again a local mechanic might have an address handy. Then visit or phone the place to see if it offers a current inventory list.

Besides this, various off-road magazines have ads from parts firms offering both new and used parts. These firms often have catalogs. And there are buyer's guides available that list firms stocking different kinds of parts for rebuilding or replacement work. In addition, you also would want to get brochures and catalogs from companies offering special parts or systems that aren't standard on production models, equipment that can add unusual features to a modified or rebuilt vehicle, including extra performance or a more sporty look.

It's helpful to know that many of these major subsystems such as engines, transmissions, tires, wheels, suspension systems and brakes, can fit a number of different frames and chassis, depending on how the design is laid out. The same chassis, for instance, could work with a slant-six or V-8 power plant of different horsepower ratings. As you're aware, or will find out if you attend races or shows featuring one-of-a-kind vehicles, some of them are made using parts from many vehicles—a frame from one type mated with a chassis from another and perhaps with four-wheel drive from still a different one.

There are a number of books in print that discuss techniques used for building or repairing vehicles in general and off-road types in particular. TAB Books, Inc., Blue Ridge Summit, Pennsylvania 17214 and Chilton Book Company, Chilton Way, Radnor, Pennsylvania 19089 have lists of their publications dealing with off-road systems that you can write for. Chilton publishes a series of repair manuals covering most major vehicle makes (but these are expensive), while TAB has a broad range of volumes available in hardcover or paperback dealing with topics like interior restoration and engine rebuilding. TAB publishes John Gunnell's *Complete Four Wheel Drive Manual.* There are other publishers of repair/conversion/modification books, including Petersen Publishing, 8490 Sunset Boulevard, Los Angeles, California 90069 and Motorbooks International, Osceola, Wisconsin 54020. Additional publishers are often found in advertisements in newspapers and magazines.

Since homebuilt vehicles are often assembled with parts from a number of different production models, it's also important to get as much insight as possible into which parts fit together easily. Hollander Publishing, 12320 Wayzata Blvd., Minnetonka, Wisconsin 55343 puts out a series of Interchange Manuals covering many aspects of the subject. A parts store or junkyard office usually has these manuals and you can consult them there.

You'll naturally want to add up the costs for candidate models to see which one, if any, might fit into your budget. Of course, if you do get into this type of activity, it probably wouldn't be something you'd figure on accomplishing in a few days or even a few months. But the cost figures could indicate the sequence of buying important parts based on your allowance, earnings or savings.

Even if you're in your teens and have a part-time job, the odds are it wouldn't be easy to complete a project of this sort on your own. But if you could arrange it as a family activity or perhaps a neighborhood program, things could go a lot faster and be a source of excitement and pleasure for everyone involved.

A rewarding aspect of this kind of project is that if you get into it, you find you're not alone, which is true both for vehicle reworking and off-roading in general. There usually are clubs around dealing with home-builts as well as off-road events. Sometimes one club may cover both areas, holding meetings, workshops and swap meets for off-road equipment, plus planning events like camp-outs, rallies and hill climbs.

Swap meets can help a great deal in keeping rebuilding costs to a minimum. At such get-togethers, people bring along extra parts or parts scavenged from an old vehicle they're in the process of reworking to trade for items they need for their projects. A swap meet provides a great way not only to get parts at no extra cost, but also to meet others involved in off-road vehicle rebuilding and modifying. Often you'll pick up how-to-do-it tips and sometimes gain access to special tools someone else might have that you don't. Assuming that by this time you've started collecting parts, you would consult your detailed parts inventory before a swap meet to figure out what you could afford to get rid of and what you'd want to get in return.

After sorting out the information and deciding on the type of vehicle on which you'd like to concentrate, it's time to sit down at the "drawing board" or the equivalent. Whether your goal is to build a scale model or design a full-size vehicle, working out the details on paper is a must. The idea is to draw up plans showing all the parts and how they'll fit together. One plan should cover the broad outline—the dimensions of the chassis and the body (assuming you're going to assemble the vehicle with a chassis from one model and body frame from another) to see if they'll meet properly and can be attached to each other. Then you'd want to do the same thing for major subassemblies—engine, transmission, drive shafts, and so forth.

The watchword is "take your time." The plans don't have to be completed in a week or a month or even a year. When you figure that dozens or hundreds of engineers at manufacturers of new motorcycles or 4×4s may take many months (or, putting all the work of engineering teams together, many man-years) to complete drawings and blueprints, there's nothing wrong with the pace of a one-person project being relatively slow. The plans you make don't have to have the accuracy of a professional group, but obviously the more precise the better. Your school shop or science teacher might be able to recommend drafting books available from the library that can help out.

If you plan to build or modify off-road systems, find out applicable state regulations. Most states have specific guidelines for what is required or permitted for a home-built vehicle to be eligible for registration. As already noted, though, off-road motorcycles don't fall under registration codes, so with these two-wheelers you wouldn't have to be concerned with state regulations. But for four-wheelers, state rules may spell out what parts can be used and the specifications for them. The place to check on these regulations is the state Department of Motor Vehicles or, for other countries, the national equivalent.

All of the tools mentioned as important items in an emergency kit for off-road operation are equally applicable for rebuilding/modification/repair work, although they form only a starting point. Things like drills, grinding machines, hoists, etc., would come into play, and special tools are needed for engine rebuilding, transmission repair, etc. The odds are you won't have these tools lying around in the backyard, but, if you have a friend who works in a garage or has a well-equipped workshop, perhaps you can enlist his or her help.

Now suppose you've built your own vehicle, or bought one ready-made or just belong to a family that owns an off-road vehicle. Where can you go from here? There are all kinds of participation activities available, ranging from club events to competitions, some sponsored by clubs, others arranged by business, civic or other organizations.

Many activities are sponsored by vehicle manufacturers themselves. Motorcycle producers sponsor off-road rallies, race and training sessions in many parts of the United States and Canada for age levels ranging from pre-teen to adult. Four-wheel-drive automotive firms in many cases sponsor even more ambitious programs including some special events that last a number of days.

An example is the Toyota annual "Land Cruiser Jamboree" sponsored by the western sales section of the company. Any owner of a Land Cruiser can take part in the event, which isn't a competition, but a chance for fans of the model to drive over challenging off-road trails and swap stories or just enjoy a short vacation.

Typically the Jamboree begins on a summer morning in August with the Land Cruisers drawn up three abreast on the main street of the Northern California town of Georgetown. After a ham-and-eggs breakfast, the drivers man their cars and take off on the first leg of a seventy-mile journey along mountain trails in the El Dorado National Forest that eventually end up winding down to the shores of blue Lake Tahoe. The goal is not speed, but to succeed in completing a demanding course whose hazards include boulders, tree trunks and chuck holes. Most of the trail is traversed at speeds of three to five miles per hour, which explains why the driving consumes most of the daylight hours of two days.

As a Toyota Jamboree organizer reported, "The course is as beautiful as it is rugged and challenging. Tall pine trees dot the mountainsides as the procession of cruisers winds along the curvy trail which once was used by pioneer settlers traveling in stage coaches. Nearly 100 years of erosion have left the trail strewn with boulders and fallen trees. In some places, it is nearly impossible to separate the trail from the surrounding landscape."

The first day ends just after the vehicles pass through the Sluice Box, a white-knuckles, boulder-strewn hairpin turn which requires total concentration on the driver's part to avoid disaster. The group, once past that, moves into the Rubicon Springs campgrounds where those who want to can go swimming in a mountain lake. Typically there's a barbecued steak dinner with music provided by a country-and-western band. The next day there's more scrambling on a winding, nerve-tingling stretch that goes steadily uphill into the Sierra Mountains before a last downhill section leads to the Lake Tahoe finishing point.

Many off-road activities are based on similar patterns, where the emphasis is placed on getting into the back country with friendly people and testing one's driving or riding skills on an informal basis. One step away from that are "runs" and "rallies." For either one of those events, the organizing group will mark off a difficult trail, not just for traveling, but for competition. The difference between rallies and runs is that the stress in the latter is on speed alone, whereas the rally is a measure of driver discipline and control.

If you were taking part in a run, your time would be

carefully clocked by the officials from the moment you left the starting line to the instant you crossed the finish line. You would be racing against the clock. The driver or rider covering the course in the fastest time would be the winner.

A rally, on the other hand, emphasizes handling and driving "sense." As set up for off-road vehicles or motorcycles, the basic principles are the same as are used in sports-car and other two-wheel-vehicle rallies. The rally organizers carefully go over possible courses, then lay out routes divided into a series of "legs." At the end of each leg, timers are posted to clock in each participant. The organizers work out beforehand what is agreed to be an appropriate time for each leg and the goal of each competitor is to complete each leg in an elapsed time that is as close as possible to the pre-established value. When all the contestants have finished the course, the judges decide the winner by calculating whose time overall is closest to the total preset by the organizers.

Another form of competition for off-road racers is drag racing. For formal racing of this kind, the arrangement is the same as for regular drag racing. In fact, some 4×4 drags are held on regular tracks. In those cases, a quarter mile is the designated course length. Two vehicles compete per race with the winner the one covering the quarter mile in the fastest time. But there's nothing to prevent anyone from setting up dirt drag courses, and more than a few off-road clubs include this on their agenda. Also popular with many off-roaders is sand dragging. As the name indicates, this is simply drag-type competition on a quarter-mile sand strip.

Obstacle races are featured at many off-road functions. The course will be laid out with a series of bumps, depressions and other formations to test driver skill. These races aren't designed to exceed reasonable capabilities of off-road vehicles. Instead, a typical obstacle course is designed to make a driver work hard to achieve a good run, but is not so severe as to pose dangers for vehicles or operators. The courses generally are set up so friends and family can get a good view of the proceedings and whoop and holler for their favorites. Sometimes there may be a series of courses laid out, each somewhat more difficult to navigate than the last, starting with one involving weaving in and out among pylons or other markers, and leading up to a layout combining a series of challenging bumps, logs and other big obstacles.

A variation on the above theme is the off-road rodeo. There's no cattle roping involved typically (though there could be, since some ranch operations employ 4×4s for roundups these days), but vehicle operators take part in a whole series of events, including obstacle courses, drag racing, finding which car can accelerate fastest over a dirt course or stop closest to an object, etc. Usually scoring is arranged on a point system, with the winner gaining the highest total for all events placing first.

And, of course, the climax of many off-road meetings is some form of hill climb. Some clubs simply take advantage of steep surfaces in the back country, while others have gone so far as to build their own special hill course. The way these are conducted can vary widely, sometimes only requiring that the operator get the vehicle up to the top of the hill for an award, other times basing the event on elapsed time or a "shootout" system where provision is made for two vehicles to vie on the same hill under increasingly difficult conditions.

The hill climb is one of the most venerable of off-road competitions. There is some argument about when the first climb took place, but the one generally thought to be the first organized event was held in Tacoma, Washington, in 1946. Since then the popularity of the hill climb has reached epidemic proportions. At this point, there are more than 100 such events held annually in California alone; nationwide, the annual number of hill climbs run by off-road organizations is in the thousands.

As we suggested, many of these climbs are part of a larger series of competitions included in a given get-together. To get some idea of what's involved, let's consider a specific annual event, the Midwest festival known as the Gravel-Rama. This is a weekend-long affair hosted by off-road clubs from three states—Indiana, Ohio and Kentucky.

Once a year, hundreds of club members take their off-road automotive vehicles, some hauling dirt bikes stowed in the back of a 4×4 pickup or on a rooftop rack for two-wheel racing or recreation, to the Gravel-Rama staging area. The meeting place is the small town of Clevis, Ohio, where the pulses of off-roaders and townspeople are quickened as each new rig rolls down the main street. Many of the vehicles bring whole family groups—parents, children, grandparents, aunts, uncles, cousins—and the relaxed atmosphere favors close rapport between club members and the local population. The people attending the festival come from all walks of life—auto mechanics, doctors, lawyers, electricians, school teachers, housewives, college and high-school students. As in the majority of off-road gatherings, the attendees represent a true cross-section of the nation.

At a given time, all the competitors get into their vehicles and the long line parades down the main street and out into the countryside toward the dirt road that leads through shaded tree-lined byways into the camping area. In the campground, the vehicles are directed by club organizers into parking areas where everyone soon is busy setting up cooking paraphernalia and tents for a several-day stay.

Everyone is eager to watch or take part in the various events. Almost as soon as a party stakes out a camp spot and finishes setting up, they rush to register for one or more of the competitions, which have been selected to provide challenging opportunities for all kinds of drivers, from novices to veterans. But no matter what the event, the utmost precautions are taken to insure safety. All vehicles entered must undergo close inspection to make sure they're in good condition, and the courses are prepared with plenty of hay bales or other sideline protection. As one attendee enthused, "The care for safety is fantastic. If this approach were taken on all of the country's roads, there wouldn't be any fatal accidents."

In this festival, the three 4 × 4 courses are: a three-quarter- to one-mile-long obstacle layout where the obstacles are typical off-road features like mud holes, bumps and potholes; a 300-foot long drag strip for side-by-side racing; and the pièce de résistance, the hill climb. The main hill climb course is over terrain with an angle of around 75 degrees and total height of 110 feet. Besides three separate race series for each course, there's also a combination obstacle course/hill climb event.

For the various events, vehicles are paired off by driver skill levels as well as by class. If this were your first off-road experience, you would compete in the novice class on dragstrip runs. You might say to onlookers, as one participant in a Gravel-Rama drag race did, "I've just learned to drive a stick shift and I'm so proud. I got the off-road fever in my blood now and I'm ready to run!"

The drag strip is on rough, if not broken, ground, and the goal is to make sure the vehicles complete the quarter mile without stalling out. If you are watching the racers go down the strip, you won't see the wild, smoking runs of pavement drags, but much more sedate operations. On an off-road strip, flooring the accelerator can quickly lead to a vehicle failure, so most competitors use only first gear with a top speed of not much above 65 miles per hour. On the more rugged obstacle and hill-climb courses, much lower speeds are the order.

Many of the vehicles taking part have received much tender, loving care from the operators between festivals. A lot of attention is given to maintenance and small changes to provide better performance. The main goal of all this, as one owner says, is to get the right engine combination, the right tires and the right gear for the course. Selecting the proper tires, he stresses, is particularly important.

Tire choice is certainly critical for the hill climb where good traction is vital. Actually, there are two hill climbs—one on a less demanding hill, the other on the large 110-foot-tall "eliminator" slope. To qualify for the big hill, vehicles must successfully navigate the smaller one and in a qualifying time.

The finals for the "super cars" are held on the second day of the festival. After the qualifying races on the first days, the evening is given over to fun and fraternization. Smoke from cooking fires rises lazily into the twilight air as families relive the day's events and exchange idle chatter about home or life in general. Later, a band strikes up to play for dancing.

In the morning, everyone is up early to get ready for the hill-climb finals. The elimination involves a series of runs, each a little more difficult than the one before. The racers begin with a fairly long approach distance to work up speed to keep the vehicle moving up the steep incline. A certain number of drivers can't negotiate the climb and drop out, after which the starting point is moved closer to the base of the hill. With a shorter run-up, it becomes harder and harder to get the necessary energy to avoid stalling out before reaching the crest. It takes a superbly tuned vehicle for an entrant to make it to the last handful of drivers. One by one, as club members lining the sides of the course or standing atop the hill shout encouragement, the last contestants find their vehicles' straining engines can't make the grade. Finally, as the afternoon draws to a close, the new champion pushes the nose of his vehicle over the top while his challenger backs forlornly in the other direction. Another festival is over, but the memories will remain—and there's always a next time.

While competitors like to place in the top three, the emphasis at celebrations like this one is on just taking part. Someone who goes down the drag strip or obstacle course for the first time is cheered and applauded just for making the attempt. As one club officer put it, "A lot of amateur sports place the premium on winning, but in off-road festivals like this one, there's no onus on losing. We have events where the main thing is just to keep going. If your vehicle breaks down, it's okay for you to just walk across the finish line. Off-roading is like a fever, but once you get it, it's a fever that can only do you good."

PHOTOGRAPHS

Seemingly perched for skyward movement in this photo, Ford's 1980s 4 × 4 Ranger pickup could well symbolize the mushrooming interest in off-road vehicles in recent years. *(Ford Motor Co.)*

Pioneer speed king and off-road driver Mickey Thompson played a major role in gaining public attention to the thrills of off-roading in the 1970s and '80s. *(Mickey Thompson)*

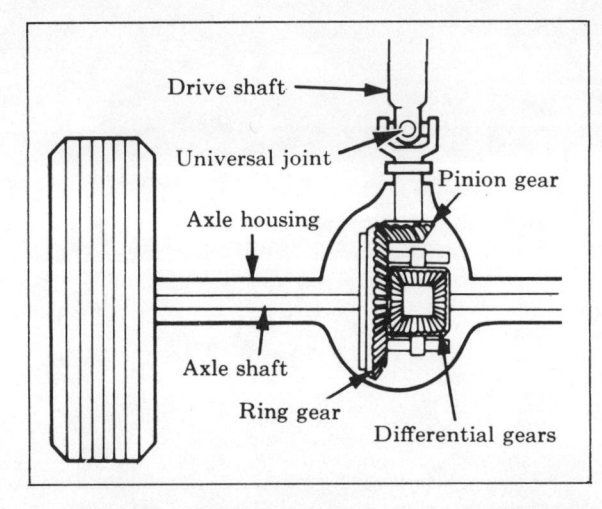

Gear systems play key roles in transferring engine power properly to the wheels in both two- and four-wheel-drive automobiles. The top diagram shows a typical differential gear design. Such a system is used in the rear axle differential of the four-wheel-drive installation shown in the lower diagrams. *(Ford Motor Co.)*

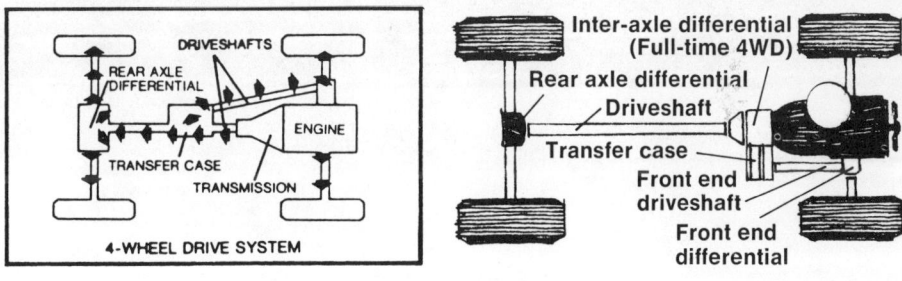

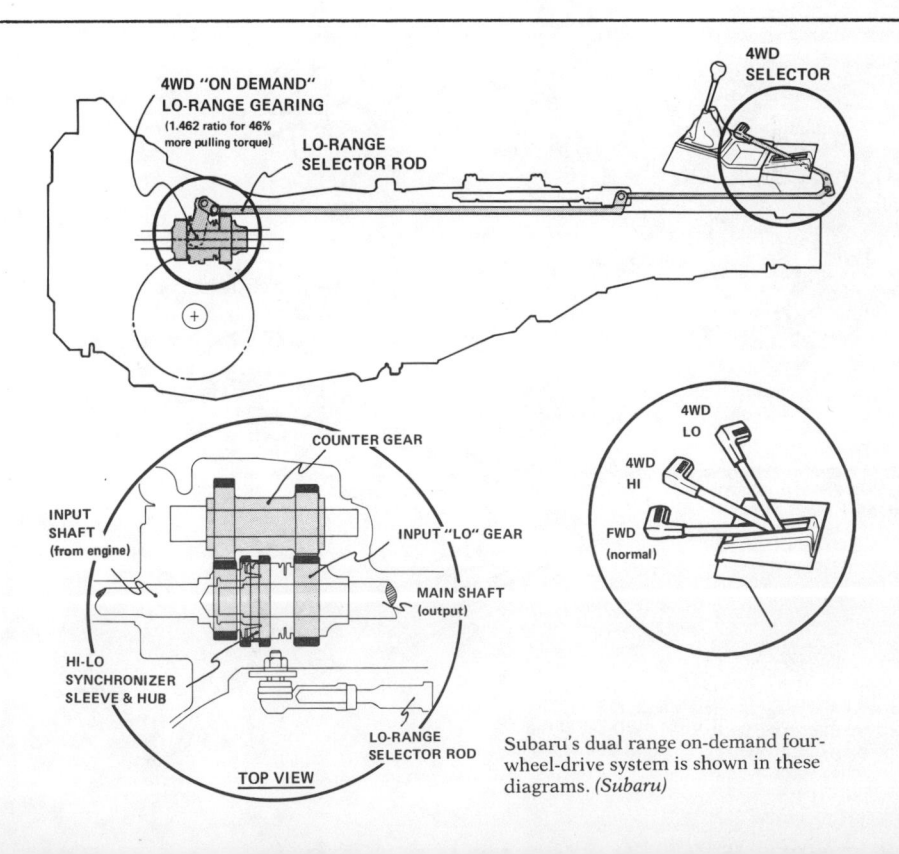

Subaru's dual range on-demand four-wheel-drive system is shown in these diagrams. *(Subaru)*

In the 1980s, four-wheel drive could be found on sleek, eye-pleasing passengers cars, such as American Motors' two-door Eagle SX-4 sedan. *(American Motors)*

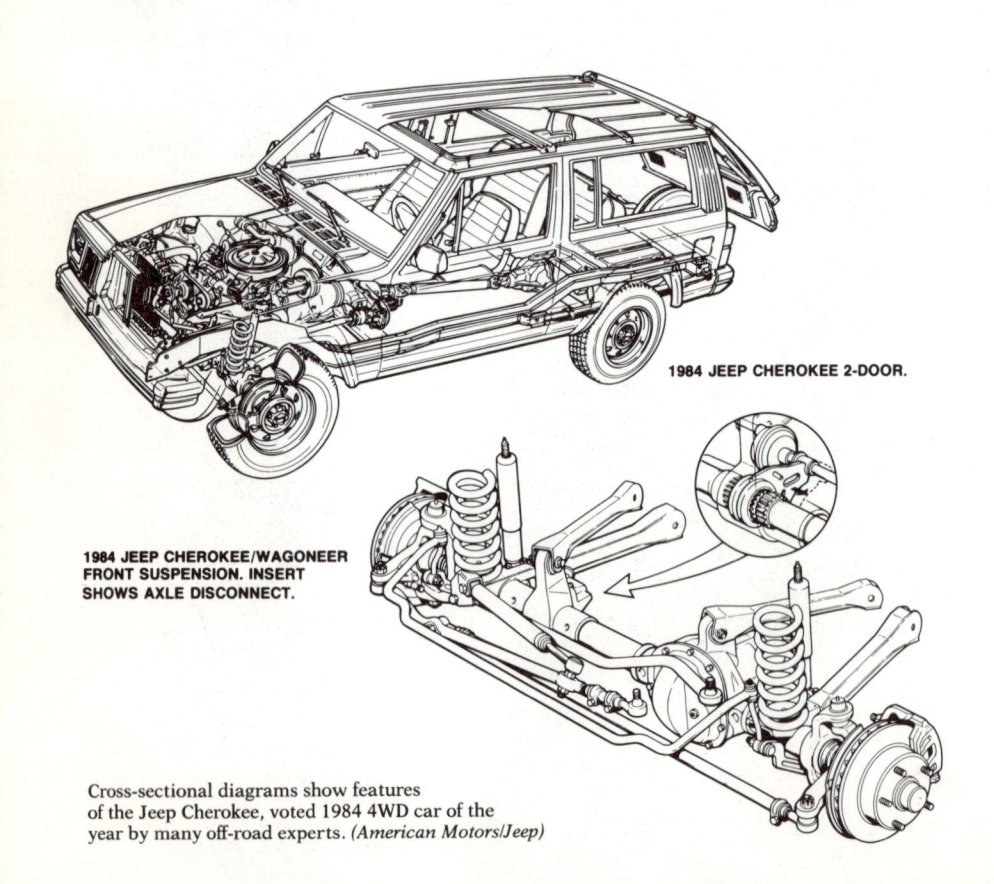

1984 JEEP CHEROKEE 2-DOOR.

1984 JEEP CHEROKEE/WAGONEER FRONT SUSPENSION. INSERT SHOWS AXLE DISCONNECT.

Cross-sectional diagrams show features of the Jeep Cherokee, voted 1984 4WD car of the year by many off-road experts. *(American Motors/Jeep)*

The 1984 Jeep CJ–7 is powered by an improved American Motors 2.5 liter, four-cylinder engine. *(American Motors/Jeep)*

Dodge favorites among off-road fans include the Power Ram Miser W150, available on a 115- or 131-inch wheelbase with either a 6½- or 8-foot cargo box. *(Dodge Corp.)*

Eye-catching design with efficient 4 × 4 performance has become a major trend among car makers in recent years. A good example is Toyota's 4 × 4 Tercel wagon. *(Toyota Motor Sales)*

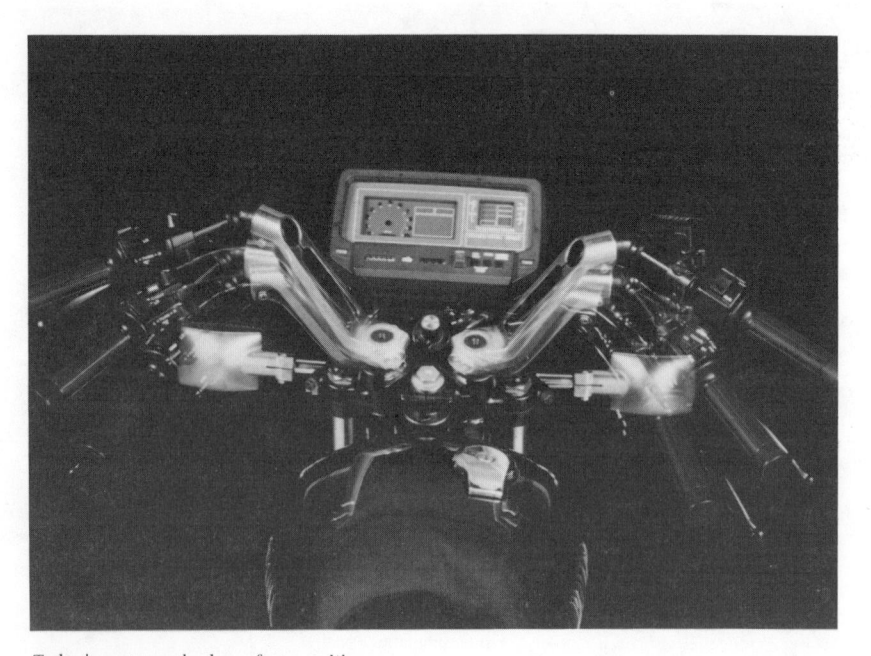

Today's motorcycles have features like variable handlebars and electronically operated instrument panels like those shown on this Yamaha model. *(Yamaha)*

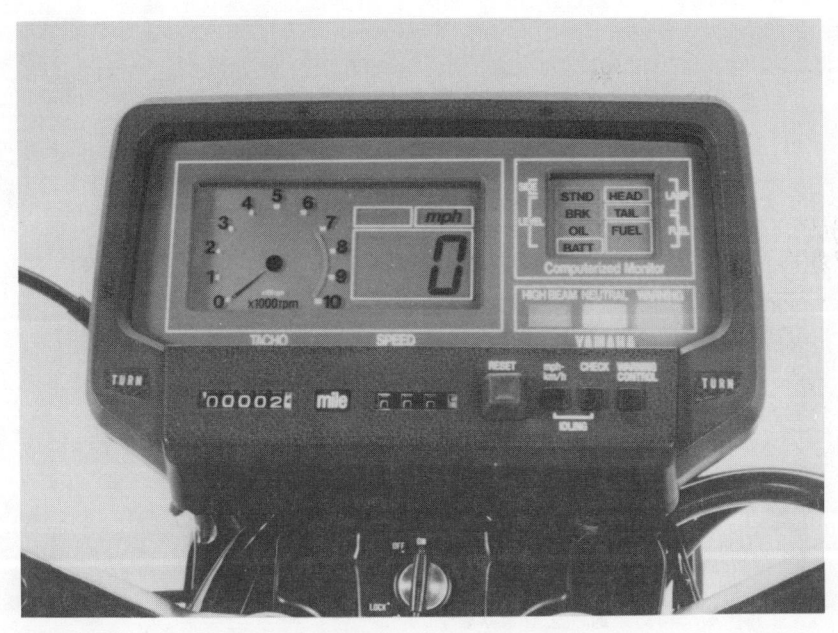

The closeup of the panel display gives evidence of the impact of electronics on new motorcycles. The display includes a tachometer and digital miles/hour indicator on the left and, on the right, a computerized monitor that can flash warnings of problems in the brakes, oil level, battery, headlights, taillights and fuel. *(Yamaha)*

Although motocross racing and off-road racing both take place, typically, on dirt or sand courses, the detailed performance needs of each in terms of shock design, types of tires, etc. is somewhat different. The model shown here is a Yamaha YZ 250 motocross. *(Yamaha)*

Suzuki's SP250 two-wheeler was designed for multiple use—trail/street/sport. *(Suzuki Motorcycles)*

Suzuki "Full Floater" Rear Suspension

Lightweight Conical Front Hub

SP-250 Engine with Dual Exhaust Pipe/Single Muffler Design

Easy-Access Tool Kit

Some of the features of the Suzuki dual purpose SP125/SP250 series are presented in these close-ups. *(Suzuki Motorcycles)*

While single-cylinder power plants were standard for most motorcycles just after World War II, the trend in recent years for both pavement and off-road models has been toward multiple cylinders. This picture presents a close-up of a multi-cylinder arrangement for a water-cooled Yamaha power plant. *(Yamaha)*

Among many Indy drivers to try their hands at off-road racing in recent years is Roger Mears. Preparing for one race, he has this Toyota mini-truck (modified by students from California Polytechnic State University) literally airborne. *(California Polytechnic State University)*

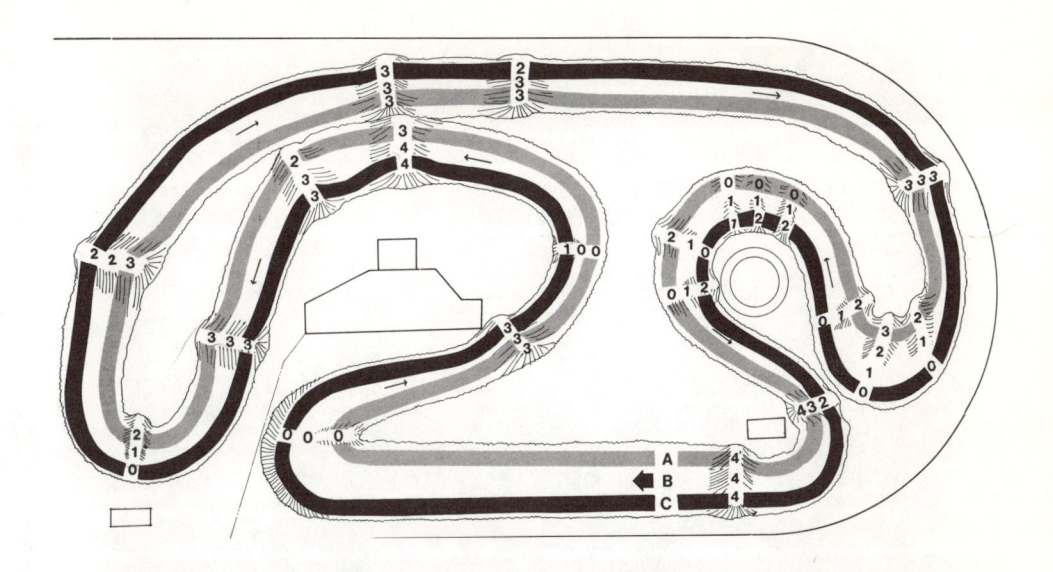

One of off-road pioneer Mickey Thompson's long-held dreams was to shrink off-road racing, in effect, down to spectator size. Here's how he did that for his Off-Road Grand Prix spectaculars at the Los Angeles County Fairgrounds in Pomona, California. The diagram at the top shows the side-by-side three-lane layout. The artist's sketch below it indicates how the layout fits into the infield of the Pomona horse racetrack. *(Mickey Thompson)*

A highlight for long-course off-road racing fans is the pre-race parade down a main street of the headquarters town. Here's one under way before the start of the Mint 400 in Nevada. *(Las Vegas News Bureau)*

Fighting his way through the desert, an off-road cyclist braces for many more miles of the same rough going. *(Las Vegas News Bureau)*

Breakdowns like this are far from uncommon in rugged long-course off-road racing. *(Las Vegas News Bureau)*

When the heavy metal monsters come roaring down the off-road racing trails, smaller vehicles try to stay well out of their way. This one, piloted by ace driver Rod Hall, is on its way to an easy victory in Class 31 in the Pernod/SCORE International San Felipe 250. Hall drove the same BPG Radial Mud Terrain T/A-equipped Dodge pickup to several other SCORE victories in the mid 1980s. *(B. F. Goodrich)*

A hardtop version of the Toyota Land Cruiser, a familiar sight at many off-road club get-togethers in the 1980s. This model is powered by a 4.2 liter (258 cubic inch displacement) six-cylinder engine. *(Toyota Motor Sales)*

After a relatively slow start in the off-road vehicle field, Ford Motor Company began to make a name for itself with its family of Broncos. A new member of the line in the '80s was the compact Bronco II. This 4 × 4 offers V-6 power, independent front suspension and ladder-frame construction on a 94-inch wheelbase. *(Ford Motor Co.)*

OFF-ROAD CLUBS AND ASSOCIATIONS

Off-Road Clubs and Associations

Across the U.S. and Canada, there are several thousand local clubs and associations dealing with all activities of off-roading. It would take a small book to list all of them and even then it would be impossible to keep such a list current since local clubs are constantly forming, merging or dissolving. It should be noted that some clubs cover only one class of vehicles, such as four-wheel drives or motorcycles, while others have divisions in most or all classifications. In addition, there are specialist clubs in each category which cover only specific types of vehicles; antique models, Jeeps, Chevy or Ford pickups, Honda motorcycles, and so on. Because of these variations between organizations, the following lists present umbrella groups which can provide you with the names of clubs in your area that accept new members and that cover vehicle types and activities meeting your particular interests.

Nationwide Four-Wheel Drive Associations

United Four-Wheel
Drive Associations
2119 South Birch St.
Denver, CO 80222
(303) 753-1464

United Four-Wheel
Drive Associations
Box 2013
Sechelt, British Columbia
Canada V0N 3AO
(604) 885-7438

United Four-Wheel Drive Associations publishes a newspaper for members called *United's Voice* that presents information on off-roading activities, including calendar listings of meetings, special events, competitions, legislation, etc. The regional association members are listed below. These regional organizations, in turn, each embrace many local clubs. It should be emphasized that there are other off-road clubs not affiliated with the United Four Wheel Drive Associations.

Alberta Four-Wheel
Drive Association
P.O. Box 65, Station T
Calgary, Alberta T2H 2G7
(403) 252-3027

Arizona State Association
of Four-Wheel Drive Clubs
2221 E. Decatur
Mesa, AZ 85203
(602) 962-4175

Associated Blazers
of California
P.O. Box 1432
Norwalk, CA 90650

California Associations of
Four-Wheel Drive Clubs
5831 Rosebud Lane
Unit M-1
Sacramento, CA 95841
(916) 338-4540

Colorado Association of
Four-Wheel Drive Clubs
2395 Wadsworth Blvd.
Lakewood, CO 80215
(303) 238-1727

East Coast Four-Wheel
Drive Associations, Inc.
c/o Skip Schaich
1324 Muhlenberg St.
Reading, PA 19602
(215) 374-3468 (Home)
(215) 378-2192 (Work)

Four-Wheel Drive Association
of British Columbia
12967-107A Ave.
Surrey, B.C. V3T 2G6
(604) 588-2462

Great Lakes Four-Wheel
Drive Association
c/o Tim Sytsma
4071 West Dickman Rd.
Battlecreek, MI 49015
(616) 964-9095 (eve.)
(616) 964-0357 (work)

Indiana Off-Road Association
3979 Willow
Hobart, IN 46342
(219) 942-2800

Midwest Four-Wheel Drive
Association
c/o Karen Schirm
3118 Howry St.
La Crosse, WI 54601
(608) 783-1187

Montana 4 × 4 Association, Inc.
Art Keene
215 South 5th
Bozeman, MT 59715
(406) 587-4132

Northeast Four-Wheel
Drive Association, Inc.
P.O. Box 65
Middlefield, CT 06455

Pacific Northwest
Four-Wheel Drive Association
946-18th
Longview, WA 98632
(206) 577-0111

Utah Association of
Four-Wheel Drive Clubs, Inc.
P.O. Box 20310
Salt Lake City, Utah 84120
(801) 250-1302

Nationwide Motorcycle Organizations

American All-Terrain
Vehicle Association (AATVA)
P.O. Box 1522
Westerville, OH 43081
(614) 891-2425

American Motorcyclist Association
33 Collegeview Road
P.O. Box 141
Westerville, OH 43081
(614) 891-2425

If you would like to form your own motorcycle group, the American Motorcyclist Association offers a booklet titled *How and Why to Form a Motorcycle Club*.

121

Nationwide Organizations—SCORE

Although originally a Southern California organization, SCORE has evolved into a national and international operation. Besides serving as official organizer of the most prestigious series of off-road races in the world, SCORE often is consulted or asked to organize many other such events inside and outside the U.S. and Canada. As part of its acronym (ORE stands for Off-Road Enthusiasts) indicates, SCORE also is active in other aspects of off-roading.

SCORE International
31356 Via Colinas, Suite 111
Westlake Village, CA 91362
(818) 889-9216

SCORE Canada
390 Chemin Du Lac
Léry, Quebec
Canada J6N 1A3
(514) 692-6171 or 692-8887

Other Off-Road Organizations

The following grouping lists both national and state organizations for different off-roading events from vehicles to racing. Some industry organizations are included. As the listing for the California Department of Parks & Recreation suggests, some state recreation departments are involved in off-road activities.

All-Terrain Desert
Racing Association
27814 Sycamore Creek
Valencia, CA 91355
(805) 254-2758

All-Terrain Racing
Association
P.O. Box 494
Apple Valley, CA 92307
(619) 247-2527

American Motor Sports
Association
P.O. Box 5473
Fresno, CA 93755
(209) 439-2114

American Sand Racing
Association
P.O. Box A
Rancho Cucamonga, CA 91730
(714) 980-3226

Arizona Desert Racing
Association
1408 E. Granada Rd.
Phoenix, AZ 85006
(602) 252-1900

California Department of
Parks & Recreation
P.O. Box 2390
Sacramento, CA 95811
(916) 322-9619

California Off-Road
Vehicle Association
5518 Colorado, Dr.
Concord, CA 94521
(415) 672-8278

California Rally Series
149 N. Rawhide
Ridgecrest, CA 93555
(714) 375-8704

Centerline Racing Series
3564 Techny Rd.
Northbrook, IL 60062
(312) 869-2434

High Desert Racing Association
961 W. Dale Ave.
Las Vegas, NV 89124
(702) 361-5404

IRA (Ice Racing Association
of Wisconsin)
370 Linnerude Dr.
Sun Prairie, WI 53590
(608) 837-9857

M/TAX Enterprises
P.O. Box 6819
Burbank, CA 91510
(818) 768-2914

Mickey Thompson Entertainment Group
53 Woodlyn Lane
Bradbury, CA 91010
(818) 359-5117

MORE
3523 Jim Wright Fwy.
Ft. Worth, TX 76114
(817) 625-8841

National Association of Mini-Truck Owners
P.O. Box 563
Mt. Baldy, CA 91759
(714) 596-5612

National Mud Bog Association
P.O. Box 2364
Glendale, AZ 85311
(602) 842-1405

Outlaw Racing Association
330 Orange Show Lane
San Bernardino, CA 92408
(714) 824-3791

Periscope Productions
P.O. Box 5652
Orange, CA 92667
(714) 639-3911

RMORRA (Rocky Mountain Off-Road Racing Association)
c/o Frank Estep
1507 E. 5th St.
Pueblo, CO 81001
(303) 544-6663 or 597-8239

Silver Dust Racing Association
P.O. Box 7380
LasVegas, NV 89125
(702) 459-0317

Southern Nevada Off-Road Enthusiasts
P.O. Box 4394
Las Vegas, NV 89106
(702) 876-0371

Specialty Equipment Market Association (SEMA)
11540 E. Slauson Ave.
Whittier, CA 90606
(213) 723-3021 or 692-9404

Sports Car Club of America
6750 S. Emporia
Englewood, CO 80112
(303) 790-1044

Valley Off-Road Racing Association
1833 Los Robles Blvd.
Sacramento, CA 95838
(916) 925-1702

Book Publishers

To find out what books about off-road vehicles and activities are currently in print, write or call publishers for catalogues.

Chilton Book Company
Chilton Way
Radnor, PA 19089
(215) 964-4729

Classic Car Club of America
Box 443
Madison, NJ 07940
(201) 377-1925

Clymer Publications
12860 Muscatine St.
Arleta, CA 91331
(213) 767-7660

Motorbooks International
Box 2, 729 Prospect Ave.
Osceola, WI 54020
(800) 826-6600

W. W. Norton & Company
500 Fifth Ave.
New York, NY 10110
(212) 354-5500

Petersen Publishing Company
6725 Sunset Blvd.
Los Angeles, CA 90028
(213) 657-5100

123

TAB Books
Monterey Ave.
Blue Ridge Summit, PA 17214
(717) 794-2191

Wards Communications, Inc.
28 West Adams
Detroit, MI 48226
(313) 962-4433

Magazines and Magazine Publishers

American Motorcyclist Association
American Motorcyclist
P.O. Box 141
Westerville, OH 43081
(614) 891-2425

Argus Publications
Off-Road Magazine
12301 Wilshire Blvd.
Los Angeles, CA 90025
(213) 820-3601

ATV News
P.O. Box 1030
Long Beach, CA 90801
(213) 595-4753

Car Exchange
Iola, WI 54990
(715) 445-2214

CBS Publications
Cycle World
1499 Monrovia Ave.
Newport Beach, CA 92663
(714) 646-4455

Custom Bike
4247 E. La Palma Ave.
Anaheim, CA 92807
(714) 996-5111

Cycle News East
4190 First Ave.
Tucker, GA 30084
(404) 934-7850

Cycle News West
P.O. Box 498
Long Beach, CA 90801
(213) 427-7433

Dismantler's Digest
1000 Vermont Ave., N.W., Suite 1200
Washington, D.C. 20005
(202) 628-4634

Four Wheeler
21216 Vanowen St.
Canoga Park, CA 91303
(818) 992-4777

Hi-Torque Publications
Dirt Wheels & Dirt Bike
10600 Sepulveda Blvd.
Mission Hills, CA 91345
(818) 365-6831

Intra South Publications
Off-Road America
P.O. Box 21436
Sarasota, FL 33583
(813) 921-5687

Off-Road Action News
9371 Kramer, Unit G&H
Westminster, CA 92683
(714) 893-0953

Old Cars Price Guide
Old Cars Weekly
Iola, WI
(715) 445-2214

Petersen Publishing
Dirt Rider
Four-Wheel & Off-Road
Pickup Van & 4WD
8490 Sunset Blvd.
Los Angeles, CA 90025
(213) 820-3601

SCORE News & Off-Road Industry Report
P.O. Box 8938
Calabasas, CA 91302
(818) 340-5750

Wright Publishing
Dune Buggies/Hot VWs
Mini-Truck
Three-Wheeling Magazine
P.O. Box 2260
Costa Mesa, CA 92626
(714) 966-2560

INDEX

AC-Delco RV Spectacular Race, 76
All Terrain Vehicles (ATVs), 16, 34, 36, 91
American All Terrain Vehicle Association, 91
American Bantam Company, 14
American Motorcyclists Association, 91, 92
American Motors, 30, 31, 32, 33, 40, 41, 63, 69
Associations, Off-Road, 20, 21
Aultman Motor Car Company, 10, 11, 12

Badger Four Wheel Drive Auto Company, 13
Baja International Race, 21, 73
Baja 1000 Race, 17, 20, 21, 23, 50, 51, 73, 77, 78–79, 81, 84
Baker, Al, 50, 51, 81
Besserdich, William, 11, 13
Bi-drive Recreational All-terrain Transporter. *See* Brat
Bilstein Corporation of America, 94
Blue Ridge Summit, 95
Braking, 59, 68, 69–70
Brat mini-truck, 34, 36
"Breakaway," 27–28
Bridgestone SCORE Off-Road World Championship, 76, 89
Brown, Dan, 36
Buddy system, 62, 91
Building off-road vehicles, 94, 96–98

Car Exchange, 93
Carlson, Timothy, 80–81, 82
Car & Parts, 93
Challenge of Champions, 76
Chandler, Gene, 82–84
Chandler, Michael, 84
Chaparral, 19
Chenowth Racing Products, 19
Cherokee, 31

Chevrolet, 39–40, 92
Chrysler, 15, 33, 39, 50
Clintonville four-wheel-drive system, 13
clothing, protective, 61
Clubs, off-road, 91, 92
Columbia Auto & Electrical Vehicle Company, 10
Columbia Automobile Company, 10
Complete Four Wheel Drive Manual, 40, 96
Conversion to off-road vehicles, 17–18, 30, 92–93
Coors/U.S.A. Off-Road Championships, 89
Cotta Motor Car Company, 10, 11
Crow, James T., 64, 66, 69
Cycle Guide, 54
Cycle magazine, 50, 54

Datsun, 33, 58, 67, 68, 76
Department of Motor Vehicles, 42, 98
Dick Dahn & Associates, 87
Dirt Bike magazine, 54
Dirt bikes, 7, 16, 43, 45, 49, 52, 59, 83
  See also Dirt-track racing; Motorcycles
Dirt-track racing, 19, 22, 87–88, 94, 100
Dodge, 39, 40, 50
Driveline windup, 28
Drop box, 29
Dune buggies, 7, 18, 19, 20, 21, 74, 75, 83

Ekins, Dave, 20
Electric Vehicle Co., 10, 11, 12
Engines. *See* Four-wheel drive; Motorcycles.
Evans, Walker, 74, 82

Ferro, Bobby, 81
Finney, Dr. W. H., 11, 12, 13
Fish, Sal, 76, 84

125

Ford Motor Company, 14, 15, 29, 33, 38, 39, 40, 68
Four-wheel drive, 7, 8. 9–17, 18, 19, 20, 24–41, 42, 43, 48, 56, 59–90
  engines, 25–26, 48
  See also Vehicles, Off-Road
Four-Wheel Drive Auto Company, 10, 13, 17, 27
Four-Wheel Drive Handbook, 64
Four Wheeler magazine, 18
Four-wheel vehicle of the year, 36, 39
Funco Race Cars, 19

Gears, 25, 26, 27, 28, 29, 30, 35, 36, 38, 44, 53, 60, 63, 64, 70–71
General Motors, 33, 39
Gravel–Rama, 101–4
Gunnell, John, 40, 96

Harley Davidson, 53
Honda, 15–16, 20, 45, 49, 51, 52, 60, 61
Honda, Hirotoshi, 50–51
Honda Soichiro, 15, 50
Hot Rod magazine, 76
How and Why to Form a Motorcycle Club, 92
Howe, K. J., 82
Husqvarna Corporation, 52, 53

Indianapolis 500, 17, 20, 21, 76, 81
Insurance, 42–43
International Harvester Company, 8, 32, 40

J–10 pickup truck, 31
Jeeps (the "Jeep"), 7, 8, 13, 14, 15, 28, 29, 31, 32, 33, 36, 38, 40, 41, 63, 64, 67, 71, 92
Johncock, Gordon, 21
Johnson, Jack, 50, 51, 81
Jones, Parnelli, 20

Kaiser Corporation, 32
Kawasaki, 47, 52
Kits, off-road, 18, 19, 92
Kudela, Bryan, 22

Land Cruiser Jamboree, *See* Toyota.
Light Truck Buying Guide, 29–30
Los Angeles Coliseum, 22, 85–86, 87, 89
Los Angeles County Fairgrounds, 87, 89

McKenzie, Scott, 18
MacPherson, Jeff, 89
MacPherson, Joe, 89
Madigan, Tom, 36, 37
Magnum family, 19

Maico 250-cc Spider, 52, 54
Mangels, Ted, 20, 77
Mears, Roger, 21–22, 74, 82
Metzeler tire, 54
Mexican 1000, 77–78
Meyers, Bruce, 20
Mint 400, 17, 20, 23, 74, 78, 82, 89
Models, scale, 93, 94
Motley, Jack, 79
Motocross races. *See* Races.
Motorcycles, 7, 8, 9, 15–16, 19, 21, 42–55, 57, 59, 61, 93, 98
  choosing, 42–55
  dirt bike vs. others, 43–44
  engines: cam, 47–49; four-stroke, 46, 47, 48–49, 51; four-valve, 51–52; rotary valve two-stroke, 47; two-stroke, 46, 47, 48–49, 51; two-valve, 51, 52; V-twins, 48
  equipment, 61–62, 63
  failures, 43, 56–57, 61
  four-wheelers, 43
  Japanese industry, 15–16. *See also* Kawasaki, Suzuki, Yamaha
  racing, 73–90. *See also* Races.
  registration, 42, 98
  surface terrain, 59–60, 65–70
  techniques and tips, 56–72; 91–104
  three-wheelers, 21, 43, 93
  tires, 54, 62, 66, 67
  See also Vehicles, Off-Road
Motorcycling magazine, 54
Mugen, 50
Munro, Stu, 42
Murray, Spence, 20

NASCAR, 21
National Off-Road Racing Association, 20
Nugent, Ted, 89

Off-Road magazine, 36
Off-Road Vehicles magazine, 36
Off-Road Championship Grand Prix, 77, 85
Old Car Weekly, 93
Old Cars Price Guide, 94
Olen, Walter, 12, 13

Palmer Speed Equipment, 19
Paris-to-Dakar Motor Rally, 21
Parker 400, 23, 73, 82, 83, 84
Passenger vehicles, 9, 11, 13, 17, 18, 24, 28, 30, 34 *See also* Conversion to Off-Road
Passive cooling, 44–45, 52
Paul, Rik, 85–86

126

Pearlman, Ed, 20
Pernod, 21, 77
Pernod Baja 1000. *See* Baja 1000.
Pernod Heavy Metal Challenge, 76
Pernod San Felipe 250, 77
Pickup trucks, 7, 9, 17, 21, 22, 24, 31, 34, 36, 38, 54, 55, 74, 83, 85, 92
Pirelli Sandcross tire, 54
Plymouth, 39
Pomona county Fairgrounds, 22, 23, 89
Poole, Ralph, 20
Power-to-gross-weight ratio, 9, 87
Power divider, 29
Publications, *See* Reference material.
PV4 magazine, 36

Races, 7, 16, 17–23, 44, 45, 73–90, 99–104
  adapting bikes to, 86
  motocross, 16, 44, 45, 75, 85, 86
  organized off-road, 19, 20, 78, 101
  prize money, 85
  See also racing classes; SCORE
Racing classes, 21, 75, 83, 85, 86–87
Rallies, off-road, 99, 100
Randall, John, 21
RC Racing News/SCORE Radio Controlled Off-Road World Championship, 94
Recycler, The, 94
Reference material, 18, 29–30, 36, 40, 50, 54, 64, 76, 92, 93, 94, 95–96
Reo, the, 11, 12
Repairs, 95–97
Rice, Jim, 43
Richardson, Kent, 81
Riverside International Raceway, 22, 76, 77
Road conditions, 65–70
Robertson, Bill, Jr., 20
Rodeo, off-road, 101
Roeseler, Larry, 81
Rose, Maury, 17
Runs, off-road, 99, 100

SCORE, 20–23, 73, 75, 76, 77, 78, 82, 83, 84, 89, 93, 94
  See also Races
Selec–Trac, 31, 32
Select–Drive system, 30
Shift-out mechanism, 28, 29
Short Course Off-Road Enterprises. *See* SCORE
Smith, Malcolm, 81–82
Smith, Terry, 79, 80
Sponsors, 21, 22, 77, 89, 94, 98
Sprague, Jim, 66

Steam-driven engine, 10–11.
  See also Engines
Step-down ratio, 26
Step-up ratio, 26
Stevens, Brook, 92
Stewart, Ivan, 74, 82, 83
Studebaker Commander Sedans, 92
Subaru, 30, 33, 34, 35, 38, 40, 41
Suzuki, 16, 51

Thatcher, Margaret, 21
Thatcher, Mark, 21
Thompson, Danny, 89
Thompson, Mickey, 7, 20–21, 22, 74, 76, 78–79, 80–81, 84, 85, 87, 90
Thompson Ridge, 77
Thompson, Trudy, 79
Three Sisters, 80
Thunder Alley, 73, 83, 84
Tools, 61–62
Toyota, 33, 36, 37, 38, 98
  Land Cruiser Jamboree, 98–99
Toyota of America, 22
Transfer case, 28, 29, 31, 32, 38, 64
Trucks, 14, 15, 24, 28, 29, 37, 38
Turner, Curtis, 81
Two-cycle engines, 15–16
Two-wheel-drive, 17, 22, 24, 25–26, 27, 28, 29, 31, 32, 34, 57, 92
  adaptation, 9, 11

U-joint system, 26
United Four-Wheel Drive Association, 91

Valenta, Tracy, 81
Vans, 7, 9, 15, 24, 92
Vehicles, Off-Road, *See* All Terrain Vehicles (ATVs); American Motors; Brat Mini-Truck; Chaparral; Chevrolet; Chrysler; Datsun; dirt bikes; Dodge; Dune buggies; Ford Motor Company, Four-wheel vehicle of the year; Funco Race Cars; General Motors; Harley Davidson; Honda; Husqvarna Corporation; International Harvester Company; J-10 pickups; Jeeps; Kawasaki; Maico 250-cc Spider; Pickup trucks; Plymouth; Reo, the; Studebaker Commander Sedans; Subaru; Suzuki; Toyota; Trucks; Vans; Volvo; Volkswagen; Willys Jeep; Yamaha. *See also* Building Off-Road Vehicles; Conversion to Off-Road Vehicles; Four-wheel drive; Kits, Off-Road; Motorcycles

Vintage Auto Almanac, 93
Vintage Chevrolet Club of America, 92
Volkswagen (VW), 17–18, 19, 20, 21, 75, 79, 80, 83, 92
Volvo, 92

Walker Trucks, 28, 29
Warren, Cameron A., 64, 66, 69
Water cooling, 44, 45–46, 52
   See also Engines

Webb, Tom, 54
Willys Jeep, 8, 13, 14, 15, 17, 32, 38, 92
Willys Overland Company, 13–14, 28
Wilson, Vic, 77

Xydias, Alex, 23

Yamaha, 16, 47, 52, 54, 57, 59

Zachow, Otto, 11–12, 13